Edward Gay

PORTRAIT OF AN AMERICAN PAINTER:

EDWARD GAY, 1837 - 1928

By

RICHARD G. COKER

VANTAGE PRESS

NEW YORK   WASHINGTON   HOLLYWOOD

For Tuck,
who urged me on. She loved the Gays,
the people and the pictures.

FIRST EDITION

All rights reserved, including the right of reproduction in whole or in part in any form

Copyright © 1973 by Richard G. Coker

Published by Vantage Press, Inc.
516 West 34th Street, New York, New York 10001

Manufactured in the United States of America

Standard Book No. 533-00777-1

ACKNOWLEDGMENTS

The author is grateful to the following authors, executors, and publishers for permission to quote from the undermentioned works:

John Fowles *The French Lieutenant's Woman.* Little Brown & Company © 1969.

James Reynolds *Ireland.* Farrar, Straus & Giroux, Inc. © 1953.

Cecil Woodham-Smith *The Great Hunger.* The New English Library Limited © 1962.

James Gould Cozzens *By Love Possessed.* Harcourt Brace Jovanovich, Inc. © 1957.

Henry Adams *The Education of Henry Adams.* Houghton Mifflin Co. © 1918.

Henry Seidel Canby *Walt Whitman an American.* Houghton Mifflin Co.

Robert Gibbings *Lovely is the Lea.* A. Watkins, Inc.

Walter Kerr *The Decline of Pleasure.* Simon & Schuster, Inc. © 1962.

Joseph Conrad, *The Nigger of the Narcissus.* J. M. Dent & Sons, Ltd. © 1897.

The author also wishes to thank the following for kind assistance:

    The Archives of American Art, Detroit, Michigan.

    Mr. Kenneth H. McFarland, Librarian, Albany Institute of History and Art, Albany, New York.

    Ms. Marguerite Mullineaux, Librarian in charge of The Albany Room, The Albany Public Library, Albany, New York.

    The Reverend Peter J. Regan, Cathedral House, Mullingar, Ireland.

FOREWORD

The head which does not turn toward the horizons of the past contains neither thought nor love.
—Victor Hugo

In *The Rivals* there is the line, "Our ancestors are very good kind of folks; but they are the last people I should choose to have a visiting acquaintance with." This is not true of the subject of this sketch. The more one learns of Edward Gay, the more one is bound to feel, "This was a great fellow; I wish I could know him."

The information on Edward Gay is quite good; on his parents and grandparents it is meager. What there is merely shows how difficult it is to account for a man and what he does.

By any sort of standard Edward Gay was an interesting man: a landscape artist of successful and satisfying accomplishment; one who savored life and had good friends, and who was flamboyant and surrounded with stories that ought to be remembered.

These stories, while known to many people, should be recorded and should be put into this account of the life of the artist. The stories are doubtless in many cases apocryphal and invented; some of them took incidents that happened to other people and put our artist into the tale as if the thing had happened to him. This was surely not necessary, since so many remarkable things did happen to him and were woven into wonderful stories. "He knew the world and its absurdities as only an intelligent Irishman can; which is to say that, where his knowledge or memory failed him, his imagination was always ready to fill the gap. No one believed his stories, or wanted any the less to hear them."[1] Both Martha and Edward were accomplished conversationalists and raconteurs, and these gifts were passed on in good measure to some of their children, who told the stories with embroidery.

If the stories are stressed, it is because through them can be shown the gaiety and the flamboyant side of the life of Edward Gay.

A study of the available records and letters has made it possible to piece together a string of facts for this account. There remains a small group of people who knew the artist well, and their recollections have been most helpful and have been freely used. Luckily also, this study has provided a number of indications of the feelings and thoughts of Edward Gay. His success as an artist did certainly come in great measure from his qualities of mind. He worked very hard all his life, using almost every daylight hour for painting. He put himself into his landscapes, but not as a figure in the picture. It is his presence, or the feeling that he has been there—in that small boat, along that path, or beneath those trees—that reveals the mind and art of the artist.

There were hard times, of course. But as Edward Gay's contemporary, Henry Adams, says, "An artist goes on painting when no one buys his pictures. Artists have done it from beginning of time, and will do it after time has expired, since they cannot help themselves, and they find their return in the pride of their social superiority as they feel it."

In general, however, the years of our artist's work were good ones for gaining a livelihood from painting. People did buy pictures, and bought enough Edward Gay landscapes to permit the artist to live comfortably and pleasantly, to be able to travel widely and frequently, and to rear a large family.

---

1. From *The French Lieutenant's Woman* by John Fowles.

Chapter I

IRELAND

> English, Scotchmen, Jews, do well in Ireland . . . Irishmen never; even the patriot has to leave Ireland to get a hearing.
> —GEORGE MOORE

Edward Gay was born near Mullingar, County Westmeath, Ireland. Mullingar is almost at the center of Ireland, lying fifty miles northwest of Dublin and eighty miles east of Galway. It is a pleasant region of gently rolling hills, entirely agricultural today with most of the land being given over to pasture for cattle. There is an Irish saying, connoting anything superlatively good: "Beef to the heels, like a Mullingar heifer." It was a good rural life in the years before the failures of the potato crop that led to the terrible famine years. In Westmeath there were middle-class farmers in addition to the small renters, and it was into a middle-class family that Edward Gay was born on April 25, 1837.

It may help to fix his birth in time to recall that 1837 was the year of Queen Victoria's accession to the throne. In that year were born Grover Cleveland, Andrew Carnegie, Whitelaw Reid, Algernon Swinburne and W. D. Howells. In that year John Constable died.

Edward Gay's parents were Richard Gay and Ellen Kilduff Gay. The parochial records of the old St. Mary's Cathedral, now kept by the Cathedral of Christ the King in Mullingar, contain the following entries:

1811 Jan. 21, Baptised Ellenor Kilduff, daughter to Patrick and Catherine Lynch,[1] Sponsors William Fitzpatrick and Ellenor Brennan.

1813 10th Sept. Baptised Rich'd Gay son to Rich'd and Mary McMorrogh, Sponsors Patrick Mauny and Elizabeth Killin.

1836 22nd June (married) Richard Gay to Ellen Kilduff. Witnesses Mick Gay and Margth Kilduff.

The baptisms of six children are recorded as follows:

1837 Edward 30th April, Sponsors Michael Kilduff & Susanna Kilduff.

1838 Susan 28 Oct., Sponsors Richard Rodgers & Catherine Kilduff.

1840 Richard 26 Sept., Sponsors William Laden & Mary Murtach. *Marlinstown.*

1842 Catherine 29 July, Sponsors Owen Kilduff & Margaret Cassidy.

1844 John 26 Dec., Sponsors James Green & Margaret Brien.

1847 Joseph 17 April, Sponsors Thomas Kilduff & Marcella Leavy.

There is no record of the other children, Eugene and Charles. They were both born after the family went to America in 1848.

The parochial records show that Ellen Kilduff was two years older than Richard Gay. They were married when he was twenty-three and she was twenty-five. Family lore has it that Ellen was a horsewoman and that she had racehorses on the land where Richard lived and raised cattle. The entry "Marlinstown" beneath the record of the baptism of Richard, Jr. is our only evidence that perhaps they lived at Marlins-

---

1. The name Lynch is honored in Mullingar because of the interest of Mr. Thomas Lynch in Catholic education. By his will of 1822 he left £600 in Government Stock for education purposes, according to the Rev. John Brady's *History of the Parish of Mullingar* (1962). Ellen Kilduff's mother, Catherine Lynch, was perhaps a niece of this Mr. Thomas Lynch.

town, a small "town-land" about one mile east of Mullingar. While Richard Gay farmed and raised cattle, his principal work was as mason and stonecutter, and apparently he was quite prosperous. "This passion for carving is not at all a new thing in Ireland. On the contrary, it goes back very far in time. Ancient cromlech and dolmen rearing out of the earth all over Ireland are carved in high or low relief. The motif is freely treated in swirls, all manner of symbols or armourial bearings."[2]

It is a bit hard to see how Ellen could have had time for mounting a horse, as the children came along pretty regularly. However, it can be fairly definitely established that the racehorses are a real part of her story. At 25 Merrion Square in Dublin are the offices of the Irish Turf Club, and there may be seen volumes of the *Irish Racing Calendar* with records of most of the races run in Ireland going back to 1800. There appears no record of horses owned by a Gay or a Kilduff, but Ellen's mother was Catherine Lynch, and one T. Lynch appears regularly as owner of horses entered in the area.

1838 Kildare Hunt Steeple Chase Wed. Mar. 14
—Mr. Lynch's ch. m. Zephyr. 5 yrs. old—
1840 Ballinasloe Steeple Chase, Mon. Apr. 6
Lynch, Mr. T., Ch. m. Isabella 6
Lynch, Mr.   br. m. Joke   7
Lynch, Mr.   ch. m. Morbucoxuoe 6
Sweepstakes of 3 Sovs P.P. to which the Stewards added a Silver Cup value 25 Sovs.
—Two mile heats jumping five four and a half foot walls. Gentlemen riders.
1840 Dunshaughlin April 22—a sweepstakes of 2 Sovs. ea. 30 added for horses the property of farmers residing within 5 miles of the Ward Hunt District. . . . and Mr. Lynch's Mountain Maid also started, but (was) distanced.

---

2. James Reynolds, *Ireland*.

1841 Meath Steeple Chase at Trim. *Meath Gold Cup* Mon., March 22—Mr. Lynch's br. m. Ruby 5 yrs. old 002 *The Trim Cup* Tues., Mar. 23—Mr. Lynch's br. m. Ruby 5 yrs. Same day *The Ladies Purse*, also ran Mr. Lynch's gr. m. Nuala 5 yrs.
1843 Kilnacreevy Steeplechase Tuesday, Mar. 13—3rd place Mr. Lynch's ch. m. Ruby 12 st. 1 lb.

The above is given in some detail because it gives background of the times. Mr. T. Lynch probably was Ellen's uncle on her mother's side. In any event, the Lynches did have racehorses, as "every man in Ireland, and most every woman for the matter of that, has 'as fine a horse as ever flittered a nostril' coming along, 'and just ready to sell, Sir; all we need is the passing of the silver'."[3]

While there is evidence of affluence and good living, there is little to tell us how it happened that Richard Gay was a revolutionary. It is true that Ireland at the time was charged with revolutionary pressures. It would be hard to find a more glaring example of man's inhumanity to man than appears evident in even a cursory reading about the situation in Ireland in the decades from 1830 to 1850. The land was held mostly in large estates by absentee owners living in England. The owner had a manager or agent to whom he looked for the greatest money return; a system of renting out portions of the great estates was developed, and this evolved into ever smaller units. The peasant renter paid his rent in saleable products, while he and his family lived largely on potatoes. When the potato blight struck there was nothing for the peasants to fall back on, since the Corn Laws imposed duties on grain which prevented imports, and all Irish grain was sent to England to provide money for the landlord owners and to build the stately homes of England.

A lead editorial in the *Illustrated London News* for May 27, 1848 says:

---

3. James Reynolds, *Ireland*.

It is difficult to exaggerate the natural capacities of the land—for grazing or for corn growing, it is almost equally admirable. It has navigable rivers, excellent natural harbours, water power sufficient to turn ten thousand mills, and to grind all the corn of Christendom; it has coal and iron, and other mineral wealth, every possible facility for becoming a great, a prosperous, and a happy country, except the facility of assured good laws, and a competent people. By some strange and perplexing fatality of mismanagement, its inhabitants have never been able or allowed to turn these advantages to any account, and have become at last the by-word of Europe, the standing reproach of British legislation, a foul ulcer, a perpetual source of disquietude and misery, setting all imaginable remedy at defiance. The masses of the people cannot be called civilized by any stretch of flattery or good nature. In those instances in which the tenant grows corn, he may not eat it. Though he rear a pig, he never tastes animal food. Though he keeps fowl, he may not eat an egg. Rent absorbs everything but the potato.

The famine years in Ireland began in 1844 and reached their worst in 1846 and 1847. Sir Robert Peel was prime minister, and he had at length come to see that repeal of the Corn Laws, which were merely a protective tariff, was essential. Repeal was finally effected in June 1846, and it ruined Peel, putting Disraeli in the saddle. The repeal of protectionism did not come in time to save the starving in Ireland, and distress increased. "In five years more than a million Irish died of starvation and of the diseases which accompany malnutrition. Eight hundred thousand Irish emigrants sailed for the United States and Canada. They took with them few possessions, but they took disease, particularly typhus, and a deep hatred of Britain. For they were convinced that it was Britain that was responsible for the appalling conditions from which they were fleeing."[4]

---

4. Cecil Woodham-Smith, *The Great Hunger.*

It is hard to describe the famine years in Ireland because all of the tragedy seems from today's perspective to have been so extraordinarily unnecessary and so much the result of greed and extortion associated with the absentee landlord and the system of the landed gentry that prevailed. It is hard for us to understand people starving anyhow, since in island Ireland one can easily reach the sea or the rivers, which teem with fish. "Huge firm-fleshed lake salmon are found in the dark depths of banshee-haunted Lough Neagh, surrounded by the glens of Autrim and the wild green fastness of the mountains of Mourne that come down to the sea."[5] It is hard for us to understand people starving without truly organizing and fighting to *take* food from their evil landlords. Actually, the people were conditioned by years of oppression to be docile and law-abiding.

Richard Gay, father of Edward, was of course much removed from the potato-eating small renter peasant. He was a farmer, on his own land, and he was besides an artisan who had in his skill as stone-cutter, as mason and builder, a separate resource. But this man became a fighting revolutionary; after the split in the Young Ireland party he associated himself with John Mitchel, Editor of the *United Irishman* and "a revolutionary, pure and simple"; and upon Mitchel's arrest and conviction (in a court with a packed jury) on May 23rd, 1848, he knew he must flee Ireland. Mitchel was convicted as "felon" and received a sentence of "14 years transportation," which meant simply that he was to be conveyed about the seven seas and held in British imprisonment, sometimes harsh and sometimes remarkably lenient, for the fourteen years. Thus did England avoid making a martyr of this man, who if he had been hanged might well have stirred the Irish to a successful fight for freedom.

Every man of Irish descent should read "that minor masterpiece," the *Jail Journal*, by John Mitchel. It is a moving nar-

---

5. James Reynolds, *Ireland*.

rative, calmly set down, where Mitchel's intense and unforgiving hatred of England shows on every page, but somehow does not interfere with the fascination of the story.

Mitchel left Dublin on the 27th of May 1848, on the *S.S. Shearwater* of the Royal Navy. We do not know the circumstances of Richard Gay's departure, but shortly thereafter he with his wife and four sons emigrated to the United States, going directly to Albany, N. Y. The two daughters, Susan, 10 years old, and Catherine, 6 years old, were left behind to come later.

The *Illustrated London News* for 1848 contains a number of items relating to Irish emigration:

The *Meath Herald* of January 22 is quoted: "Numbers of small farmers, holders of twenty acres and under, both in Meath and in the adjoining county of Cavan, have already commenced to make preparations for the Spring emigration by disposing of whatever interest they may possess in their farms. It is anticipated that the spirit of emigration will this season be very widely diffused; in fact, it is no longer confined to the struggling farmer or the bankrupt tradesman—there are numbers occupying a most respectable position in society to whom such thoughts a short time ago were foreign, but who now begin to cherish the prospect of doing more in America or the colonies than they can ever hope to accomplish at home. This spirit, if widely extended, as we have every reason to believe, will prove highly detrimental to the country."

Again, in the issue dated November 4, 1848: "The provincial journals contain further accounts of the progress of winter emigration, chiefly to the United States. Most of the emigrants are farmers who had been in comparatively comfortable circumstances. Besides those proceeding from Irish ports, many are going over to Liverpool to take passage from that port."

Also, in the issue of November 18, 1848: "Emigration from Waterford, Cork, and Limerick proceeds with vigour.

In Dublin the desire to try their fortune in the New World has very generally seized on the small trading class, and they have an organization for the establishment in America of a colony derived from home. A number of shop-keepers, alarmed by the prospect of the times and the little hope of improvement which presents itself, have agreed to emigrate in a body. They have purchased a small territory in the District of Wisconsin, and thither they propose to proceed, and found, perhaps, a city. Each will leave with a sum of £ 2,000 at least, either in cash or merchandise. The Guild of Bricklayers and Masons of Limerick have appealed, through the public prints, to the humanity of their townsmen for contributions to a fund they are raising to enable their active and unemployed members to emigrate."

We have no information as to why Richard Gay took his family to Albany, N.Y., to set up a new life. The deciding factor was probably letters from friends or fellow masons who had earlier gone to Albany. In any case, Albany proved a good place for the boy Edward, arriving there at the age of eleven, to enjoy his boyhood and to be guided into manhood and into art.

Chapter II

ALBANY

O tempora! O mores! (What a time! What a civilization!)
—CICERO

The family of six, the parents and four boys, apparently went directly to Albany. The boys were Edward, Richard, John and Joseph, and their ages were eleven, eight, four and one. Two girls were left behind in Ireland: they were Susan, aged ten years, and Catherine, six. The ocean crossing was made in June 1848, which was just ten years after the crossing of the Sirius, the first steamship to cross the Atlantic, sailing from Cork. Where Richard Gay and his family sailed from and on what ship, we do not know.

What a time to come to the New World! It was the year that gold was discovered in California; it was the year that Wisconsin was made a state; it was the year that the United States acquired from Mexico the territory embracing New Mexico, Texas, California, Nevada, Utah, Arizona, and parts of Colorado and Wyoming. In Europe it was the year of the Fall of the Bastille, of civil wars in Germany. In 1848 Marx and Engels published their *Communist Manifesto;* John Stuart Mill finished his *Principles of Political Economy;* Thackery's *Vanity Fair* came out, and Balzac completed the hundredth volume of the *Comédie Humaine.* In art, the Pre-Raphaelite Brotherhood was formed in Rome by Holman Hunt, Rossetti and Millais.

Shortly after the family got to Albany there occurred a disastrous fire. On August 17, 1848 the most densely populated part of the city burned, with some six hundred buildings being lost. The Great Fire swept both sides of Broadway north of Herkimer Street, burning over 37 acres of property including the Eagle Hotel, and was not stopped until it had done over three million dollars worth of damage. The city had a population of 62,000, and after the fire there was rapid rebuilding. Richard Gay was a stonemason of competence and experience, and he easily found work. He apparently became a builder, since affluence came fairly soon.

In 1848 the leading hotel was Congress Hall, and "Congress Hall Block" became the site of the State Capitol, built in 1886. The capitol grounds were bounded on the north by Washington Avenue, on the east by Park Place, on the south by Congress Street, and on the west by Hawk Street. In 1862, according to the Albany Directory, Richard Gay, mason, lived at 32 Congress Street. It also lists Edward Gay, landscape painter, at 3 Lafayette Street (his studio, apparently) and noted that he boarded at 32 Congress Street. The O'Reilly telegraph line, connecting Albany with New York City, had been opened in 1850; at the time of the 1862 Directory, Richard Gay, Jr. and his brother John are listed in 1866 as telegraph operators at Broadway and State Street.

It is interesting that the home at 32 Congress Street looked out on the Congress Block, as did also the studio occupied by Edward Gay in 1866 at 64 Hawk Street, Arbor Hill. The house on Congress Street had a parlor with green carpet and horsehair furniture and gave an impression of a prosperous family.

Our best information on the early life of Edward Gay in Albany comes from the account written in 1921 by his wife, Martha Fearey Gay. This will be quoted in full, with minor editing. It begins:

> Sometimes he told curious tales of his boyhood in Albany. The family had left Ireland, really fled from Ireland when John Mitchel was convicted. Edward Gay later hated the word "Fenian," and you may surmise

that his father was a revolutionary. Not only Fenian, but even his Irish beginning he tried to hide. "I am an American," was his word about himself, and this remained his attitude through life.

All of the five brothers went to work, little fellows, as they all were to earn daily bread in a new land and grew up silent boys in their home, as if indeed they were fugitives. The mother had no sympathy with the cause which had torn the father from her loved home and the cattle and the racehorses which had been her portion on the lands of Richard Gay in Mullingar.

She spoke Gaelic by her own fireside and had a store of family lore and was kind to beggars. To be torn from it all for what? So she sat very still often with hands in her lap, and the day might go by without a word. The bitterness passed into her children's lives for none of them were like the sunny-faced Irishman, their father, whose ideals remained the breath of his life; revolutionist, reformer in old Dutch Albany.

We may insert here some hindsight comment from the perspective of a hundred and twenty years. As for the "I am an American" attitude and trying to hide his Irish beginnings: we must remember that in 1850 the Irish were some 40% of the foreign-born population of the U.S., and that most of them were recent arrivals:

> . . . the term Irish Catholic meant the base and the obscure vulgar. Few had anything that could be called education. Their mostly low standards of living—all they could afford—resulted in objectionable habits and manners. Politically, they were a troublesome mass vote at the disposal of their own highly purchasable politicians. Religiously, they seemed to be the willing dupes of their priests, of a superstition to the Protestant mind corrupt and alien.[6]

---

6. James Gould Cozzens, *By Love Possessed*.

So it is not surprising or shameful that the boy growing up should wish to hide his Irish background. As a man he never spoke with an Irish brogue—though he could do so—and he seldom told Irish stories. Just one comes to mind, and that a brief one, what we would call "a quickie." This story has to do with the belated racehorse that also ran; at the end of the race the owner, Patrick O'Brien, put his arms about the horse's neck and with infinite compassion whispered, "What detained ye?"

Richard Gay was indeed a revolutionary. He had been a revolutionary in Ireland and his rashness made him a fiery reformer, as Martha says, even in Old Dutch Albany. In the year after his arrival one of the recurring cholera epidemics, this one the worst of all, struck the city of Albany: in June 41 cases were reported; deaths 22. In July 343 cases and 125 deaths. In August 345 cases and 150 deaths; in September 37 cases and 23 deaths. Richard Gay had been trained in the seminary, though he did not become a priest. He worked with the sick, and when people died in the streets he administered extreme unction, which he had no right to do. Another story has it that he mounted the pulpit in the church and denounced the clergy for their neglect of the sick and dying. Whichever story is the truth, it is known that for his action, rash though humane, he was excommunicated. Real effort has been made to secure details about this incident, but it appears that the Catholic Church refuses to release information about excommunications. Perhaps this is a wise position.

Certainly for Edward Gay as a boy of twelve, the disgrace to his father must have been deeply traumatic, and our knowledge of what happened helps us to understand why he chose to hide his Irish descent. He grew out of it, for in 1882, when he was established as a landscape painter, he served as chairman of the committee sponsoring an exhibition and sale for the benefit of the Irish Famine Fund. The leaflet bulletin was as follows:

Artists' Picture Sale
for the benefit of
The Irish Famine Fund
Leavitt's Gallery
817 Broadway, New York

Committee

Edward Gay   Chairman
Geo. H. Story   M. DeForest Bolmer
A. C. Howland   Wm. Whitlock

The Artists' Exhibition and Sale for the Benefit of the sufferers from Famine in Ireland will open this Thursday evening, March 25th at Leavitt's Art Gallery, 817 Broadway and remain open, day and evening, Four Days, until Tuesday, March 30th; on each night at eight o'clock, they will be sold at auction.

You are requested to attend the Opening, and also the sale on Tuesday which promises to be one of the most important of the year, apart from the general interest which its object will ensure for it.

Then follows a list of no less than 73 names of artists represented. It is apparent that Edward Gay and his committee did a good job.

To return to Albany, Martha's 1921 story is further quoted:

Some of the children went to school. They were choir boys, to be sure, in the Cathedral, and picked up a little Latin, they being eager for knowledge, and music was familiar to them.

Edward Gay must have been attractive in appearance, so easy was it to get a place where others congregated. He was a boy in a familiar bowling alley, a page in the Assembly at the Capitol and when at length

Narcisse Rémond who ran the Marble Pillar wine cellars, installed him behind the counter he soon developed such a gift in the mixing of drinks that the old Frenchman gave the youth the freedom of his wine caves. To pour wine in such proportion into color and sparkle that it should tempt old men and young, seemed a strange gift for one so young who never himself had a desire to taste.

It was in these wine cellars, their stone walls freshly white-washed and lighted from above, that Edward Gay began what was to be his profession. A stick of charcoal in his hand wherewith to keep the tally of wine bottles opened, in some moments of leisure he drew upon the walls a landscape that had held his fancy. Faint lines at first, then, as he grew bold, a charcoal sketch of real vigor, and another sketch followed it. Rémond came down to see what detained the fellow, but the Frenchman had the instinct for art. "Eddie, Eddie, you must study art! It is no longer that you mix drinks for these beasts who have lost the taste for wine—my vintages." Edward could not give up his job, as he was the eldest of the children at home.

Then came the summer. The gilded youths who frequented Rémond were planning a camp at Lake George. Rémond was to provide their liquor. The old Dutch aristocrats of Albany dined with pomp and their sons imitated their taste. Drunkenness was a common failing among the aristocrats. Indeed, the most brilliant among these youths, Van Rensselaer, Talbot, Kidd, Ten Eyck, came to an untimely death in the height of their beauty. Edward knew them all, had opened the Frenchman's choicest vintages at their call, so that when Rémond suggested that Eddie go with them to Lake George to serve them, he knew so well how between meals he would have time free to sketch (for indeed the youth was a genius).

It was all settled. Rémond had introduced him to James Hart and the boy had spent the noon hour often in his studio. Between them he got his outfit and his first summer of sketching, with James Hart to criticize. The revels of the brilliant camp he served did not deter him. Extended by day, his easel was set up before the fair summer and he looked out on the nature he loved.

One night rowing these youths in from a wild visit to William Henry, he stopped their carousing by laying down the oars. Afterwards, remembering, he spoke of their charm—their brightest promise. The summer was very good for Edward Gay. He had constantly associated with a fine grade of man, young and bent on draining life's fullest cup, while on their part they admired his work.

In an exhibition of post-impressionism, long years after, there hung a canvas by (B?) entitled "Ponies and Young Men." In a grove on a sunny field stood tethered ponies, at their bridles stood young men, naked, life thrilling through every fibre of young men and ponies alike. Something such perhaps was that summer of unbridled fancies and the race to be run. At Mt. Delphi on the heights there still remains the long line in stone where the runners toed. For centuries past no runners essayed that long distance looking toward Parnassus, but the line remains where eager runners awaited the signal. In the soft Grecian air you seem to catch in echo the signal and with foot on the ancient line hear, "Be off!" With the runners was Edward Gay, that summer at Lake George.

There were to be ten years of academy work including the two years' study in Germany, his marriage, the birth of his boys, before he left Albany and took a studio at Doddsworth's in New York City. Albany held its group of artists. Foremost among them were the sculptor E. D. Palmer and his young students, C. C.

Calverly and that genius Lamont Thompson. There were perhaps twelve who were to become academicians. Among the painters were James and William Hart, the older men, while George Boughton was just beginning, and Homer D. Martin, and happy among them all, Edward Gay. Old Twitchell and Elliot, the portrait painters, and William E. Paige were among the Albany artists.

Martha's story does not tell how or when she and Edward Gay met but it must have been shortly after the summer at Lake George. In addition to his work at the Marble Pillar he taught a sketching class at the Albany Female Academy where Martha Fearey was a student. She was five years younger than he and had come with her parents from Steventon, England in 1844. Already beautiful at sixteen, Martha was a petite blonde with a wistful air, but active and full of fun. At school she was called "Sweet Corn," for her corn tassel hair. Edward Gay was captivated. They read together "The Culprit Fay," by Rodman Drake, a "new poet" who has been quite forgotten.

He was studying in the studio of James McD. and William Hart, and by 1860 he had painted "The Mountain Stream," his "first important work"—pretty good for age twenty-three. In that year too Edward Gay's name appears in Martha's small autograph book, with pen and ink sketch of the moon above a hillside, the date April 3, 1860, and in beautiful printing the verse:

> Naught is heard on the lonely hill
> But the Cricket's chirp and the answer shrill
> Of the gauze-winged Katy-did.

Also, in the little book are three small photographs, one the three-quarter face with hat, one a profile looking to the left, and one full face, both of these without hat. All three were apparently made on the same day.

The next record of the courtship is a note written August 30, 1861 from Catskill to Martha (not Mattie), with a pencil sketch of our young artist done by J.S.J., a member of the party. This shows him with gun and sketching portfolio, striding along in high boots. The note invites Martha to come to his studio—to see the sketches that he had made on the trip; it is worth recording, especially for the light it throws on how at age nineteen Martha had "set her cap." Here is the letter:

> I have just returned from the wild, wild woods and am reading your letter (which, by the way, I expected *'ages ago'*) and in trying to answer it I am so sorely perplexed with the many things which I wish to say that I think I won't say anything, for before you receive this I will be back in Albany—and just look at what a figure I'll cut. J.S.J., one of our party, did me up so today before leaving the camp, so I will lock myself up in my studio for three or four days 'til I mount all my sketches and get a little of the *tan* off! Then I will be ready to tell you how to do "those trees"; and as I intend that *you* shall be the first who shall see my sketches, will you please drop a note in the post office and let me know if you would like to call at my studio between 3 and 5 P.M. Then perhaps I will be able to answer that queer question, "if it is possible for two happy—," let me read again; ah, yes, "if it is possible for two to be happy?" No, that is not it—so queer this that I can't read the sentence right. Well! When I see you I will get it right, so—
>
> Edward Gay

Chapter III

KARLSRUHE

To take what there is, and use it, without waiting forever in vain for the preconceived—to dig deep into the actual and get something out of that—this doubtless is the right way to live.

—HENRY JAMES

The Albany Directory for 1862 showed that Edward Gay had a studio at No. 3 Lafayette Street, and he was listed as "landscape painter." In the same year he went to Germany to study at Karlsruhe with Johann Wilhelm Schirmer (1807-1863) and Karl Friedrich Lessing (1808-1880).

We do not know how the young artist managed to find the money to make the trip to Europe, but it is fairly reported that Martha's father, Thomas Fearey, helped. This was possibly because, although he liked the young man, he did not at all like the idea of his beautiful golden-haired Martha marrying an Irish Catholic, an artist. Thomas Fearey was a Baptist of very strong religious feelings; he was also a businessman and no doubt he felt it a sound investment to contribute to a fund to send this young man far away. Other contributors to the fund were possibly Rémond, and James and William Hart, for each felt that he had discovered this new talent. Certainly Edward's father, Richard Gay, had become somewhat well-to-do, as is evidenced by the portraits painted by Asa W. Twitchell. These companion portraits, oval and framed in good square-to-oval gold-leaf frames, are of Richard Gay and his wife Ellen Kilduff Gay.

Typical of the period, they are over-dark, yet they are good, sound portraits. Richard, with ruddy cheeks and luxurious beard that left his chin bare, appears a jolly fellow. Ellen is in a black dress and is as sour as Martha's story depicts her. Twitchell lived in Albany and was an established portrait painter; according to the minutes of the Albany Common Council, he was paid $1,000 each for his portraits of Reuben Fenton, John T. Hoffman, and Samuel J. Tilden, Governors of the State of New York, in the period from 1865 to 1877. The fact that Richard commissioned these portraits tells us that he was reasonably affluent and able to send his gifted son to study in Europe.

Why to Germany? Why to study with Schirmer and Lessing? The explanation is easy, since Edward Gay was a protégé and a student of the Harts. These two Scottish brothers had lived in Albany since early youth. William was self-taught, and had himself taught his younger brother James. They were well established landscape and animal painters, both having become members of the National Academy a few years earlier. When these successful painters took him into their studio about 1860 they were delighted with their pupil; by 1862 they felt he was ready for further study in Europe and they sent him to Karlsruhe to Schirmer, with whom James Hart had studied ten years before.

A small daguerrotype shows Edward Gay seated with James Hart standing beside him. At twenty-four he has no moustache and no beard. A small oval portrait by Twitchell, painted at about the same time, shows him with black hat and billowing black hair. A year later in Karlsruhe he had the beginnings of the moustache and goatee that he was to wear for the rest of his life. A pencil sketch, signed "Peter Schirmer," shows him before the easel with one of his teachers. His curling hair falls over his ears and over his collar.

What of the two teachers? Each of them was some thirty years older than Edward Gay; each was established and successful as a painter of historical landscapes. Schirmer had studied under Schadow at the Dusseldorf Academy, and had concentrated on historical scenes until he fell under the influence of Lessing and became a leading landscape painter in the style of Poussin. He was a professor at Dusseldorf, and in 1853 became director of Karlsruhe Art School. He was a member of the Berlin and the Dresden Academies.

Lessing, a great-nephew of the writer, seems to have been the stronger personality as well as the better artist of the two. He had been a pupil of Rösel and Dähling at Berlin, then of Schadow at Dusseldorf. In 1830 he became director of the Dusseldorf Academy at age twenty-two, being a prodigy in a time of prodigies. In 1858 he became director of the Karlsruhe Gallery.

Thus the two men seemed to have the highest qualifications. Yet in the light of today's judgments there were in Paris in the year 1862 vastly better teachers and a vastly better milieu. In 1860 there had begun the loose federation of the group whose work produced the movement called Impressionism. News of the new excitement had not reached America, nor would it have true impact there until years later when Durand Ruel showed the new work to New York. A Swiss painter named Gleyre, even less known than Edward Gay's teachers Schirmer and Lessing, and certainly with lesser credentials, had a studio in Paris where in 1862 his pupils included Manet, Renoir, Bazille, and Sisley. Gleyre's teaching is said to have aroused resistance which drew this group together and sent them to join Manet, who had turned away from the realism of the great Courbet.

It is easy to think of the possibilities of "what might have been" had Edward Gay been sent to Paris instead of to Karlsruhe, and had he fallen into the excitement of the little group of men in Gleyre's studio. It might have been wonderful indeed, or on the contrary it might not have worked for Edward Gay. The fact is, he was apprenticed to sound, experienced, conventional, historical landscape painters, and he was ready to learn technique and style, but without adopting it. It is true that in writing to Martha he was discouraged and complained that he was accomplishing nothing, that he was wasting his time. Yet the two teachers were perhaps not as bad as Martha's indictment. She describes Edward Gay's fascinated enchantment when he first saw Constable's pictures on their visit to London in 1881. She says, "This gamut of color, cool, clear green and delicate prisimatic grey wiped from his mind all the harsh insults of his German study." This was Constable, who had died at sixty-one in the year that Edward Gay was born. This was Constable who had gone back to nature, back to painting out of doors, but without falling into the mysticism and detail that entrapped the Pre-Raphaelites when they came along in 1848. Edward Gay was indeed perceptive when at forty-four he studied Constable. But, and this thought cannot be avoided, he should have seen Constable nineteen years earlier, as did the Impressionists in Paris; and he would have, had he gone to Paris instead of to Karlsruhe. Appreciation of John Constable's painting was greater and came sooner in France than in England, where the grand and mystical Turner was acclaimed by the romantic taste of the time.

In Karlsruhe Edward Gay learned how to paint his darkling fields with open skies. He learned much else—a love of opera, a working knowledge of German, and the joyful friendships of youth. A letter from the young German couple that he lived with gives a warm picture touched with schmalz. The envelope, postmarked 1 March 1865, is addressed to Wohlegeboren Herrn Eduard Gay, No. 81 Hawk St., Albany, New York. The letter, all in German, is written in "Latin" script (not German script), but is nonetheless hard to read. In translation this is the letter:

Karlsruhe, February 1865

Dear Mr. and Mrs. Gay:
  I enjoyed reading your letter and was glad to learn

that you are still alive and altogether with your loving wife; however, I am sorry that you lost your father through death.

Dear Friend, before we received your picture from Mr. Consul Duncan, my wife was of the opinion that you had died, and I always replied that this could not be true. I want you to know, that as long as I live I will not confess to myself that you should die, and should I have to die soon then I shall ask God to give you the age of 80 years. Since we parted in Mannheim I have been concerned as to how you fared on the remainder of your trip.

The day after you left us, I found a book, written in English with pictures, which I brought right over to Mr. Consul Duncan because you told me that he is going to see you again in Ludwigshafen. I also wrote you a letter with the thought of saying goodbye again; however, I was afraid it would not reach you in Ludwigshafen and so did not send it.

Now the weeks have passed one after the other and it is already a year since your visit. Your life is now so embellished because of your loving Martha of whom you were dreaming and speaking of your love while here in Germany.

Gustav went home last September and now we have a boy here from Bremen who is attending the "Politechnicum." We are all doing fine, God be praised. However, we did not get a chance to take some pictures, but we shall do so as soon as the weather improves, and then send you and your loving wife a sample too.

If God is willing then we will get an addition to our family sometime in May or June. Because my wife wishes so, we have ordered a girl! On November 12, last year, Julie married Noe, and we were all together till three o'clock in the morning. Also on New Year's we were together and thinking of you.

Dear Friend, you are asking me whether I was ever doubtful of you; surely not! I am doubtful about many people but never about you. Therefore, I would like to congratulate your wife that you are surely a good example of the male sex. Had you not been so, then we would not have accepted you though you were a member of the family.

Please let me say thank you for your invitation to visit you. However, my business does not allow me such a trip at the moment and as a result I am more anxiously awaiting your next visit.

Unfortunately, I cannot remember the amount of that bill you are asking me about, since the book in which it was recorded does not exist any more. However, my wife thinks that it was 52 fl 34 x or 54 fl 34 x.

I hope you do not mind my bad writing, but writing in "Latin" gives me quite some difficulties.

Finally I send you a thousand kindest regards, also for all your relatives, and remain

Your friend,
George Däubert

Also many regards from Noe and Julie
Auf Wiedersehen

> *Füllt die Gläser bis zum Rande,*
> *Freunde stosset an*
> *Denn es gilt dem brävsten Manne,*
> *Gilt meinem Freunde Gay.*
>
> *(Fill the glasses to the top,*
> *Clink the glasses, friend;*
> *Then it is for the bravest man,*
> *It is for Gay, my friend.)*

Chapter IV

MARTHA

> *You look at a star from two motives, because it is luminous and because it is impenetrable. You have at your side a softer radiance and a greater mystery, woman.*—Had anybody said to him, "Do you desire anything better?", he would have answered, "No." Had God said to him, "Do you desire Heaven?", he would have answered, "I should be the loser."
>
> —Victor Hugo

We now come to the most delightful parts of the story of Edward Gay, and that is the two lovely and touching love letters that Martha Fearey wrote to him on August 16th and 20th, 1863, while he was at Karlsruhe. These are written in pencil in a tiny script on small notepaper. One cannot even be sure that they were ever dispatched to the lover across the sea. Here they are, in full:

August 16, 1863

Dear Soul:

Last night I came home from such a glorious trip, that I am to tell you about presently, and sat down in the sitting room to recount to the people all my adventures. Very busily I was talking when Sadie put in "Oh, Mattie, by the way, there is something for you, but now mind you, go on," so on I went talking for a couple of hours I guess, of all the wonderful things that had happened—when at length she produced a *letter* and from *you*. I concluded I had about finished all I had to say: I sat me down in my little room; and now today your letter is all finished. I have dreamed over it, slept with it wrapped up in my little pillow, and I would I were of all women the truest and noblest that I might write you the answer I so much desire to write. Angie said to me when I saw her a fortnight ago, "Think, Mattie, what a worker he is, what a brave earnest worker!" Ah, Edward, I am very proud of it, and your German life serves to me a little breathing space that discontent and trouble should not enter into; if you did not do a particle of work in Germany—I cannot see that these years would be in any respect a failure. I know how much better you will work when you come home, with how much surer foundation and how much clearer sight. Now when you come home you are to be a great painter. Nature will open its secrets to you and you shall translate its sunny meadows, its forests and all the mystery of its waters. I think of all lives the artist's should be happiest—and you speak in your letter of your "queer temperament" now so overflowing with happiness and then "lost" and "miserable." You are gloriously happy, I know; when you work aright and for the unsatisfactory moments that *must* come there is patience which is peace. It may be I was constituted so especially happy that I might be of some advantage to you; that is a very pleasant thought, to me. Your letter that I woke early with under my pillow and took out and began to read again lying there, and then fell asleep at something you had written about Annie Main. I think I never asked you anything about your past life, though many and many the stories people have told me of it, yet I never cared to know whether they were true or false, so little did they affect my feeling with reference to you. The years I have known you I am content with knowing of. You will tell me all of them some day.

August 20, 1863

Mine Own Edward

I have begun so anew because I feel so very bright, so very happy. You too must be glad. Do you know what a wonderful letter yours was to me? How ever since my heart has been altogether laden with joy? Do not ever think but that you can make me happiest, you are very good, very good to me. I only want to stand by you and tell you it, to tell you I wish my hair were an Undine's tresses that it might be worthy, that it is all yours, that I am all yours, that in your heart you could not hold another love than mine, could not, Edward, though my "rivals" were fair. Then I have much else to say to you. Your maiden with the brown curls took up a half a sheet of your precious letter—selfish maiden. Some day when you see the wondrous wine held up before you, the Rhine wine, Schiller's inspiration, you will know someone will look at you a little sadly should you drink. Yet, Edward Gay, I am not afraid to trust you. Ah, dear, you have not forgotten your old ways as I almost dreamed you had, so quite had your letters differed from our evenings, half-tease and half-earnest. I am *wild* to see you. You do not know anything about it how I run from kitchen to the top of the house and down again, the wildest scamper, Mother wondering meanwhile at her crazy girl. When I think of that day so surely to come, when you will be home, surely to come, I say, you are holding my hands telling me you are with me, come back to me.

Now I must tell you of my happy summer days, all in due order. We started one evening in the boat for New York; delayed in starting we had all the morning hours on the river—and those hours are my summer idyl, a faint crescent moonrise soon to be lost in the dawn as sunrise lost in the palpitating mist centering all its soul on our blest sloop, my golden ship lost in the drowning mist. But O my earth it found itself again, found its pearly inlets and the sun found them too, how it disdained its grey mantle of fog; how the proud mountains thrust it back and threw it off, and O the glory. So we opened our "summer book" with illuminated pages, Lottie and I. From New York we went out to sea, cast anchor out of sight of land past the golden line of the far-off beach, and swung with the will of the sea—how we counted the distant sails, watched them near or be lost on that silvered sea beyond—and there came while we looked a steamer from Europe. Some day there will come in, just so, another steamer, and on it will be my heart. I am waiting and watching over the silver sea. Ah! but we had a storm at sea, thunder and lightning cloudblackness, and after it the splendor of the sunset— more still I must tell you. Afterward we camped out on the highest peak of the Catskills. Eight of us went, toiled up the weary mountain and on its summit forgot to be weary. How I laughed; I could not be still. The world had one happy soul in it that day that stood on the mountain cliff, exultant. Then we lit our campfire in the sunset, a gypsy fire cheery enough in the cold mountain air, and we girls got the supper ready—such a supper and such hungry bodies! Then afterward I went alone to watch the stars, on a rock at the brink of the precipice under the wondrous dead pines, all laughter had flown there with that heaven so close to me—I learned how to pray that night—God was close by and a spirit soft but sure spoke to me, "If you want *anything* ask it now." I think I did ask for a high soul, for, so much for you and me Edward, pray. We wrapped up in shawls and lay down in our tents, and slept till the sunrise, the sunrise on the rolling mist that tossed below. Saturday evening we reached home, and then, as I told you, your letter was waiting—had been waiting five days. It made my week almost perfect. How well

I am, how joyous I am. I think I never was so well before—walk—how I can walk—and sit still I cannot. Before I had time to finish my answer to your letter I started off again; two days I have had at Cedar Hill riding. On such beautiful rides, and sailing and singing my peace song. Now home again, but Monday Annie Buel and I start for New Hampshire, a week's pleasure, and then Cambridge and my work. Now you will know of my summer—know that the next is when this lacked to be perfect. Darling, darling, I know less and less every day how to get along without you.

I heard yesterday that James Wands, you remember him, was shot before Port Hudson. It seemed so sad, so very sad. My two cousins have had, one, his arm shot off, the other his hand; brothers they are. You ask after my work. I have painted a little picture since I came home—the best I ever did, it is, but very poor at that. It troubles me a little to have you think of my painting while you are away, for you will come home and be disappointed in me, I fear; I never loved painting better than I do this moment and I have looked and thought all the summer with reference to painting in the winter. You will think it is no good without work; the time for work is to come. Have I told you of Helen Lanner, another friend who paints? Portraits—principally, and how she loves it and how she works! I grew brave in watching her. I have sketched little this summer and that little I think I shall never show you, for I know just when it is poor and why poor—without your telling me. Do you know I always was terribly afraid to show you my work. I never had the faintest idea of my own with regard to it because it was all merged in what you would think and would say. So it is better to have you away. I am deciding for myself, becoming a little less dependent in the little I do. I met Mr. Larit of Cooper Institute a few weeks ago. We had a wonderful talk on painting and love. I had an idea he was an earnest old man and found him a young enthusiast, and so beautiful. I have a letter from Laura Osbour who is painting this summer. She mentions that Mr. and Mrs. Palmer, James Hart and George William Warren are spending the summer at Aurora—twelve miles from Auburn. All that is showing at Annesly's at present are some larger paintings of Clinton Loovidge's. Miserable—entirely miserable.

The letter from George Däubert mentions Consul Duncan, who was American consul at Karlsruhe. He and Gay became fast friends—such friends that when Gay's first son was born he was named Duncan, after this friend. Consul Duncan was from Newberry, S.C.; and it is evident that he was one Southerner who was content to view the Civil War in the United States from a distance and in a safe berth in Seward's State Department. Of course, many Northerners were not caught up in the struggle, and our Irish artist least of all; but it is perhaps worth noting that Henry Adams was in London as an innocent dilletante "secretary" to his father, who was the American ambassador.

While Edward Gay was at Karlsruhe, something happened that was a shock to our twenty-six-year-old student artist. This was the sudden death of Schirmer, the elder of his two teachers. Edward Gay continued working with Lessing until the spring of 1864. At the end of June he sailed for home. He first went to Ireland, where he met his sister Sue and Kate Kearney, a cousin, and he brought them with him back to Albany. The only record of the trip is the pastel iceberg picture inscribed "For Mattie," signed and dated July 1864. We do know that it was a rough northern passage, and that they were forced to land at Montreal and their fare was paid by the steamship company for them to go by rail to New York. All this is known only because there was a railway accident in which none of the three were hurt. The steamship company awarded Edward Gay a cash settlement, amount unknown. He accepted it, but for years afterwards he felt twinges of conscience for taking something he should not have taken. The story goes that Kate Kearney got a sewing machine—presumably purchased with the payment to her.

Edward and Sue had just reached Albany when their father, Richard Gay, died July 25, 1864. No details exist, other than a line in Joel Munsell's 1867 *Collections on the History of Albany from its Discovery to the Present Time,* where on page 205, under notes from newspapers of 1864, it states, "July 25: Richard Gay died, aged 60." Since the Mullingar record says he was baptized on 10 Sept. 1813, this would have had him baptized at nine years old, which would have been most surprising. It was usual to baptize within a week after birth; if we assume Richard Gay was born in 1813, then he died at the age of fifty-one. It is not surprising that he had no elaborate funeral, since because of his excommunication he could not be buried by the church. He was probably buried in the public cemetery on the hill north of the city.

For our Edward Gay things were happening pretty fast in 1864. On September fifteenth he was married to Martha Fearey. She was born in Steventon, Bedfordshire, England, and had been brought to America by her parents, Thomas and Sara Porter Fearey. Thomas had taken up his trade of bootmaking in Albany and had prospered. He had set up a successful business of manufacturing shoes and was making shoes for the the Union Army during the war years.

Edward Gay and Martha were married by the Baptist minister; afterward the young couple went to the priest to be married, as Edward did not feel he was in fact married without the sanction of the Catholic Church. The priest was broadminded and he reassured them, saying a Catholic marriage was not necessary, that the "hearth" was the most important thing. Thus Martha never felt she must bring up the children as Catholics. This unusual position taken by the priest was perhaps because of the excommunication of Edward's father, so recently deceased. Apparently the reassurances of the priest were welcomed by both bride and benedict. The young couple were, to be sure, beyond the reach of mundane or religious considerations at the time, and plunged forward happily into their life together. News of their doings is scarce, but we think they lived with neither set of parents but at once rented the studio at 64 Hawk Street, Arbor Hill; two years later they lived at 1 Clinton Avenue while Edward Gay still had the Hawk Street studio.

These were war years, and an interesting letter shows our young artist's interested but unconcerned reaction to the war. It seems that in June of 1865 with Martha's younger sister Lottie he visited Martha's brother Thomas Fearey (also slightly younger than Martha at Bailey's Cross Roads, Virginia, where the brother-in-law was stationed with the Union Army. This seems to have been a kind of lark: and we should remember that Edward was 28, Thomas was 21, and Lottie was 19. The letter was written by Thomas H. Fearey to his father, with envelope addressed to Thomas Fearey, Esq., Albany, N.Y. It is quoted in full:

Bailey's Cross Roads, Va.

June 8, 1865

Dear Father:

We have just come in from a horseback ride—Lottie is putting off her habit. She rode my pony "Jack" and could not have done better. She will make a graceful rider, I think—Ed and Lottie arrived safely on Wednesday evening, just in time to see the review on Thursday. I had given up seeing them for I sent an orderly to Washington twice to get any telegram that might come, but he returned without.

I was out inspecting my party, preparatory to review, when an orderly from Army HeadQ's rode up with an envelope which proved to be a telegram—

that was 6:30 P.M. I immediately ordered my horse and went to the city—they came at 10:20. As I had to be back at Hd.Q's at 6:00 next morning, I returned by moonlight, arriving at Hd.Q's just as reveille was being sounded.

Next day the review passed off very pleasantly. The General invited us to his house and there we partook of an excellent lunch. After that I sent my horse back to camp and stayed in town till the next afternoon when we rode out here. Today we have been on a long ride in Gen. Wright's light wagon.

I have my application in for a leave of absence, and hope to go home with Lottie and Ed. We propose to ride to church tomorrow, and then I hope to get a room nearer our own Hd.Q's than this house. But this is a very pleasant house. Mr. Gay is very much exercised after his ride, for his horse trotted hard.

We have had a pleasant shower today which has layed the dust and cooled the air.

We rode about 20 miles in the carriage and five on horseback today.

Ed says, "It's gorgeous," Lottie, "She's satisfied," and Lieut. F. thinks Martha ought to be here.

    Your son,
               Thos. H. Fearey

(And in a different handwriting, this P.S.):
Maj. Gen. Fearey, Comd'g Home Forces—

I have the honor to report that in obedience to your order of the 7th I have reconnoitered the enemy's lines visible from Munson's Hill—and find "All quiet on the Potomac."

    Your Obed't Servant
         E. Gay
        Pvt. Brig. Gen'l
        In the Field

It would appear from the above that Edward Gay was on very good terms with his father-in-law, and with his in-laws generally. Martha could not make the trip, since she was to have her first child a fortnight later: Duncan was born on June 23, 1865. Their second son was Ted, and he was born the following year.

We return to Martha's 1921 story:

Subjects of pictures are strangely misleading. Was Raphael aware when he painted LaFornanine that it was the tints of lovely flesh under that jewelled robe, or when he painted the Madonna, now in Dresden, that it was the green of the shawl about the young mother's shoulders which would beguile the eyes of generations to come? Lovelier canvasses were never painted. Yet, when Wyant painted the mountain stream or Childe Hassam his "Spring," they too would make of pigments an irrefrangible light. Down in the pearly morning flow the swift grey waters of Wyant's streams, while on Childe Hassam's canvasses stroke by stroke his facile brush begs you to linger as after a tale that is told. The young Irishman, Edward Gay, whose career as an artist we are following, was to paint before he had seen pictures. His education began before the windows of Annesley's Art Shop in Albany where hung in those early days the canvasses of Durand and James and William Hart. He saw Durand's "Recollections of An Old Man"—a wide pastoral scene filled with all the details of a farmer's life. Over all those crude details broods an atmosphere that remains in memory.

The artists one by one left for the greater art center in New York. How easily Edward Gay did it. He packed his household goods and put them in the attic while we left for a summer of sketching in Vermont. At the farm house in Arlington where he found board the lovely Sawkill ripples on the other side of the road, there Edward Gay caught trout for his breakfast. There were other boarders, and before the summer was over one of them, Dr. Brown, had invited us, babies and all, to return with them to their home in New York to stay while Edward Gay found a home and a studio. This inconsequent artist's family traveled to the great city, found an apartment at 860 Sixth Avenue and a studio in the Doddsworth, sent for their household goods and were soon established in the city of their dreams— and Dr. Brown had brought them.

There were symposiums evenings in the back shop of Annesley's Art Store. It was a notable group, so many were to achieve greatness. Old Albany sat on its hills with the Hudson River at its feet. The family of Henry James had just left for New York, but the preacher, William James, Sr., still preached in random pulpits his astute philosophy. There too was Blandina Dudley, their aunt of the "Haunted House" where Isabel visited, whose "Portrait of A Lady" Henry James was to write. Blandina gave her wealth to build the Dudley Observatory. Already it stood on the Liboli Hill, a thing of pride, and already the West Shore Railroad was laying its tracks across to Trivoli Hollow and presently finished. The vibration from the trains was to destroy the permutation of the stars. The Observatory was moved.

Dr. Brown used to look in on us, loving our sculptures and pictures, propounding some questions to little Duncan and holding in his arms the baby Vivien, who came to us from the stars, he thought. Then he would send for us for his Madrigal rehearsals, and old English songs became familiar in those early New York days. Dr. Brown was the leader of the Madrigal Society, and was an ardent lover of music. When the scourge of cholera reached New York, the elder Putnam publisher was his patient, and Ansell, the artist, from whom he took the germ. The three dear friends and lovers of music soon lay dead together.

Edward Gay was soon made A.N.A. of the National Academy, with his picture "The Suburbs" well hung in the exhibition. It seemed as if his way to fame stretched plain before him. In that picture, "The Suburbs," a gleaming city lay in the distance and seemed to be upon the countryside. There was a certain nobility in the canvas, very simply achieved as of the inevitable, and the Academy recognized it and hung the picture well.

When they had lived two years in the city it was the same Dr. Brown who urged them to find a home in the country, for the baby was ailing. Edward Gay found a little place in Mount Vernon.

In the seclusion of his country studio his hand had learned the choice of many a touch. He painted unaware, and out of long, quiet hours grew those still canvasses which marked the ardor of the painter. He had lived in his youth through that time when the Pre-Raphaelism first broke upon the art world. Had he not subscribed for the New Light? And had he not seen the exhibition of Moore and Hill, American brothers, and read "The Form," edited by Ruskin, which brought the canvasses of Rosetti, of Burne Jones into such favor? The period passed; like childhood in its happiness, Holman Hunt was but a name. Charley Moore had become a professor at Harvard and Ruskin had reclaimed for England those thousands of water colors by the great Turner, who was further from pre-Raphaelism than any English painter.

The foregoing was written by Martha a great many years after the events recounted in her story. She was seventy-nine years old, but her memory was surprisingly good. We need not agree with all of her comments on art, but we should not too readily disagree, either, since accepted ideas on art and artists change with the passage of time.

It is plain that the years in New York were fun for Edward Gay and his wife; and that they were productive years for him is evidenced by his election as Associate of the National Academy of Design in 1869, at age 32. He was, as Martha says, on his way, and it did seem that his way to fame stretched plain before him. As things turned out, however, there were many obstacles and many disappointments, despite happy achievement all along the way.

Chapter V

FOUR THIRTY-FOUR

> *This is the true nature of home—it is the place of Peace; the shelter, not only from all injury but from all terror, doubt, and division.*
> —John Ruskin

While Martha's story tells us that the good Dr. Brown urged them to move to the country for the benefit of the ailing baby Vivien, she does not mention that another baby was expected. The apartment at 860 Sixth Avenue was already crowded with the three small children, and it just would not do. It was Martha who did the real urging that persuaded Edward Gay to look for a place in the country.

He found a place in Mount Vernon, in Westchester County; and the place proved so right, and so good a choice, that we are the more convinced that our artist was lucky as well as smart. The old Dusenberry farm had been cut up into lots and streets had been laid out. The Dusenberry house itself then fronted closely onto the extension of South Second Avenue, and it was this house that Edward Gay bought and moved his family into in the year 1870. The house, originally a very narrow one, had been added to on the south side. The addition comprised a living room and parlor with ceiling higher than in the low dining room and kitchen across the stair hall, and above the new higher rooms were two fair-sized bedrooms. These rooms were each reached from the narrow upstairs hall by going up four steps that were miserable and hazardous, but there is no record of an accident. The living room had a bay window looking east to the street, and French doors led to a south porch covered by an arbor for grapevines. There was a fireplace with a white marble mantel, and sliding doors opened into the smaller parlor which had a similar fireplace and windows looking west to the garden and the barn.

The older part of the house comprised a low-ceilinged square dining room on the street side, a kitchen and scullery and woodshed behind in the manner of a New England farmhouse. Upstairs in this north side of the house there was a front bedroom, a small bedroom (later converted into a bathroom) and a large room above the scullery. This room became the studio, since it had a good north window. There was a white picket fence along the street, and a young elm tree had been planted to the right of the small front stoop.

There were five pear trees in the yard, a grapevine over the south porch, and a climbing rose at the flagstone terrace outside the door at the back of the hall. The lots to the north and to the south were vacant, and Edward Gay leased them, so that there was room for the children to play, so that they had also the fruit from the great pear trees to the north. These trees obstructed the light to the studio windows and had to be heavily pruned, but the lease on the lot made this possible.

The following description of the garden is in Martha's handwriting; it is not a part of her 1921 story: "The air, heavy with the odor of honeysuckle, is the charm that has set me dreaming of the Mount Vernon garden. Over our piazza these July days the rich vine riots, its golden pipes distilling honey of fragrance for each passerby. We do not begin to know the gardens that make ours a city of homes, but there's my own—I invite you in. One long path leads to the back gate which leads no whither but has a clump of hollyhocks, faint yellow hollyhocks in stately bloom to guard it. The carriageway wanders under an arch of syringa, curving around the southwest sides to our little chalet of a stable. Over its roof the grapevine is full of fruit. My rows of beans, of peas, and of corn give us something for every day. The long wing kitchen looks out on a trellised dooryard. At the door an old-fashioned single June rose is fair with its last flowers. I remember gathering baskets of roses from that same vine the first June so long ago when I came to Mount Vernon."

It was a beautiful place, and just right for them. Although our artist lived out in Westchester, in the country, and some twelve miles away from Manhattan, he felt himself still a New Yorker, and still in the center of the art world. He had just been made an Associate of the National Academy and was a regular contributor to its exhibitions as well as to those of the Watercolor Society. He exhibited in 1869 "Swabian House," in 1870 "Late Afternoon." These were sold, the latter to J. H. Johnston, the jeweler at 150 Bowery. Johnston became a staunch friend, of whom more will be told later.

So things were on the upturn. But there was, as there always is, something to worry about. That something, for Martha, was money, and she was concerned about her prodigal husband.

Edward Gay was in demand as a master of ceremonies for artists and other stag dinners. He appears to have been a ready and convivial companion. Martha begrudged spending money for whisky, since the family grew larger and it was hard to sell enough pictures to provide for them. She cleverly proposed to her husband that he make an agreement with her that he would not buy a bottle of whisky except when he sold a picture. He agreed when she said that she herself liked a "wee drop," but felt they could ill-afford it unless a picture was sold.

Well, they weren't easy to sell, and our poor artist suffered through a dry time.

Then one day he came home with a bottle. Martha welcomed him at the door. "Oh. you've sold a picture!"

"Yes," he said, without enthusiasm.

"What picture?" she asked.

"Oh, the little cherry orchard."

"Oh, a fine one! And what did you get for it?" Looking somewhat glum, he said that actually he'd not sold it, but had traded it for a piece of ground. "Wonderful!" she cried. Nothing could be better—she had always wanted to own property.

"Well," he said, and "Well" again, and he was not sure that she'd be happy about this property. What was the matter with it? she asked, and finally he admitted that he had exchanged the little picture for a lot in the cemetery!

There was a pause, and finally Martha said, "Open the bottle, we'll drink to a long life!"

And that is the end of the story, or perhaps not quite the end; for the lot in the cemetery of old Eastchester Church south of Mount Vernon was not used for some fifty years—save that the sexton did bury his little daughter there. On discovering it Martha said, "Never mind, it will be all right."

Of the family, and mind you there were nine children, the first to be buried there after 58 years was Edward Gay, who died on March 21, 1928; and the next, just three weeks later, was Martha.

Martha had asked her son Duncan, in a letter written in 1921, to arrange for a "headstone of fine marble with carved top perhaps, at your discretion," and upon which would be carved her name, and that of our artist, and with the final line of Milton's "Lycidas"—"Tomorrow to fresh woods and pastures new!"

The "headstone" is a marble bench "for lovers," apparently a later idea of the ever-romantic Martha. It was designed by Duncan, and he had it made. The "fresh woods" inscription is there, and on the back and on the arms are cut the names of the children: Duncan, Will, Helen and Patty. Old Eastchester Church is a beautiful church dating from 1765, and the cemetery slopes away from the church to the south. Beyond are the great gas tanks and the embankments of the railroads.

There are other stories that have to do with whisky. Edward Gay was Irish in his appreciation of "a glass," and he not only felt no shame, but he seemed to think he should show the world how he felt. This was perhaps because of his hatred of any sort of pretense. There is the story of the grandson and "those Baptists"; it will appear later. To be told now is the story of how Edward Gay came upon his sixteen-year-old eldest son busy with empty whisky bottles that he had brought up from the cellar. Duncan, with a clever technique involving a file and a heavy cotton cord soaked in alcohol and tied around the girth of the bottle and set on fire, was making cups from the bottom part of the bottles.

"What are you doing?" the father said sternly.

"Why, I am making jelly glasses for mother," the boy replied.

"Well," said his father, "stop it, and put those bottles back into the pile in the cellar. I like to know where my money went!"

It was many years later, during Prohibition, when a friend—a true friend, truly—sent him a bottle of scotch, and the old man, needing help in drawing the cork, called upon his son Will to help. Will pulled the cork and poured out a very generous portion, sipped and savored it, and then drank it, saying he had to test the whisky, that there was no telling what you'd get in these days. The old artist said, "Son, my dear, I just don't trust you!"

The baby that arrived soon after the family was settled at Mount Vernon was called Helen, named after her paternal grandmother Ellen Kilduff Gay. From her earliest years Helen seemed to have an intellectual bent and to be endowed with Irish wit.

The family was busy with the four children under six.

There was a German servant who did all kinds of household work and taught the children their ABC's in German: Ah, Bay, Say, Day, etc. All their lives both Vivien and Helen remembered.

Edward Gay worked hard, using every daylight hour. He painted and sketched out of doors when the weather was good, and worked in his back-room studio at other times. He retained his contacts in the city, cultivating his friends there among the artists and the dealers. A friend—an affluent friend, no doubt—took him to dine at Delmonico's, at Beaver Street and South William Street. This was the most famous of all of the great New York restaurants, and our artist had not been there before; yet he was not one to be awed or to be overly impressed—all good things, he thought, were made for him.

The friend ordered asparagus. Edward Gay had never seen it before, but tackled it bravely; his friend saw that he was eating the large end of the stalk, and nudged him and said, "The other end!"—to which he somewhat haughtily replied, "How do you know but what I prefer it?"

It was at another visit to Delmonico's that he first saw caviar. Never afraid to ask questions, he inquired of his host, "What is caviar?"

The host, with suave savior-faire, said that the question should be answered by an expert, and he called the headwaiter. He said to him, "My friend Gay here has asked, 'What is caviar?' Can you tell him, please?"

Whereupon the august headwaiter spluttered, "Caviar French, caviar Italian, caviar English, caviar Rooshian," and spreading his arms in a gesture embracing the world, concluded, "Caviar!"

Edward Gay served as master of ceremonies at a dinner at the Salmagundi Club in honor of the great African explorer. As the port was served at the end of the dinner the explorer passed around a packet of loose uncut diamonds. There were twelve diamonds in the packet, but when it had made the round of the table and was returned to the owner, two diamonds were missing, and of course the explorer, along with everyone else, felt badly about the situation. Search on the table and under the table failed to find the missing gems. There was discussion as to what to do, and the president of the club finally said that he felt they should call the police to inquire into the case. However, he said he would not do so unless everyone present would consent to being searched. Not many liked this idea, but all reluctantly agreed—all but one, our artist, the master of ceremonies. He flatly refused, giving no reason but being greatly affronted. So the matter was not pursued, and the party broke up on a somewhat unhappy note. Of course, the diamonds were later found—they had fallen into a salt cellar. It was years later, in recalling the affair, that one who had been present at the dinner said to Edward Gay, "Why did you refuse to be searched? Why did you make such a fuss about it?" To which he replied that he thought the suggestion improper, and that beyond that there was a more personal reason: Martha was at home and was not well, and the partridge was so very good that he had wrapped one in his napkin and had put it into his inside pocket to take home to her.

With all his sociability Edward Gay soon entered into the life of the village community. He organized a rifle club and built a target range at Bronxville. This was one of the few sports that ever interested him. However, after a few years the target practice drew complaints from neighboring homes and the club was disbanded.

Mount Vernon was a village, and Edward and Martha soon had a broad acquaintance and good friends. There was Joseph Wood, who went to Europe with our artist some years later. There were the Dellenbaughs and the Blackmores, and David Pell Secor, and many others.

Edward Gay in these years played the violin. He had learned while in Germany, and he could entertain with snatches from *La Traviata* and other operas. Another ability, a strange one perhaps: he was an accomplished ventriloquist. A family story tells how the children were all at supper when the doorbell rang. Duncan went to the door, and the children all heard a boy asking for "a bit of cold vittles."

In 1872 another baby arrived. This was Charlotte, always called "Peepin," and often referred to as "Peepin, who vanished." She died when she was three years old, being the only one of ten children that did not live to maturity; most of them indeed achieved a remarkable age. There is a small panel of children running up a green hillside; behind the group is a wraith, the tiny "Peepin." On the back of the panel is the verse,

> Oh the babble of the children,
> Oh the flurry and the fuss,
> To begin with Cain and Abel
> And to finish up with us.

When the family occupied the house at Mount Vernon, Edward Gay seems to have rented it for a time, as it was not until a year later that he gave a mortgage for a face amount of $862.50 to Mary A. Dunsenberry. He seems to have paid this off with proceeds from another mortgage to one Hugh Porter which he was still paying on five years later. He often traded with friends for various pieces of land. He bought from Mr. David Pell Secor a triangular lot at First Avenue and First Street, a good value near the New Haven Railroad. This he sold in 1887 to help his daughter Vivien when she won a scholarship to study architecture at Cornell. She was the first woman student of architecture at Cornell. He was very proud of her.

It was David Pell Secor also who traded the cemetery lot for the little picture, and who gave Edward Gay the holograph of "My Country, 'Tis of Thee."

A lot on the east side of First Avenue that the artist had bought was sold in 1874 to Thomas Gay. Thomas Gay was a cousin who was headwaiter in the famous dining room of the Fifth Avenue Hotel at the corner of Fifth Avenue and Twenty-third Street, where our artist was often master of ceremonies at dinners. It is likely that he had a part in getting this business for his cousin, for many of the annual dinners of the Artists Fund Society were held there, and contributed to the great popularity of the Fifth Avenue Hotel as a place to dine.

Edward Gay was working hard, exhibiting regularly: "Ready for the Reapers" in 1875; "Late Afternoon Near Albany" at the Philadelphia Centennial Exposition, and a "Quiet Hour" in 1876; "The Slopes of the Mohawk" in 1877. The eight-year-old eldest daughter, Vivien, was taken to the Philadelphia Centennial, and she always remembered most the "Woman made of Butter," a work of sculpture that she saw there.

The village of Mount Vernon was a pleasant place to live in the eighteen-seventies. There was a large German settlement in East Mount Vernon, and the good German people brought concerts of singers and chamber music. There was an enthusiastic group of people who had formed in 1872 a club called the Mount Vernon Athenaeum, its object being "The cultivation of literature, music, elocution, art and the promotion of social acquaintance." Members were men and women, and the meetings were planned in detail and printed programs were prepared. One of these was as follows:

THE ATHENAEUM

Will meet May 17, 1876 at the
Residence of Mrs. Gay

Centennial Guests

Semiramis,	Assyria, B.C. 2000
Miriam,	Palestine, B.C. 1500
Sappho,	Greece, B.C. 600
Aspasia and Celon,	B.C. 450
Cleopatra, } Chasmian, }	Egypt, B.C. 30
The Lorelei,	
Dante's Beatrice,	Italy, A.D. 1320
Iseulte of Ireland,	
Kate Carney,	
Joan D'Arc,	France, A.D. 1430
Highland Mary,	
Queen Catherine,	England, A.D. 1530
Priscilla,	America, A.D. 1630
Olla Podrida, Coffee	

G.A. FOWLER, SEC.

It is recorded that all of the above who came in costume were represented by women, with the exception of Edward Gay who represented Sappho—he wore a long Grecian dress, a band around his head, and a mask. He carried a roll of baggage with "Troy" imprinted on it. There is mention of his fine acting and the remark that his feet showing beneath the robe were the only stumbling-block. These meetings of the Athenaeum were great social affairs, at once much fun and of intelligent intellectual stimulus. They were well attended, sometimes with as many as forty people present. This was education and serious culture, but fun.

A word about the final item in the program, the "Olla Podrida, Coffee." We are told that a member had proposed that at the conclusion of each meeting the club would have "Olla Podrida," giving as an illustration of what he meant: "Take any object, a chair for instance, and discuss for five minutes the wood, the style, period, comfort, etc." The Olla Podrida on coffee was held on the night of May 17th; and before the members left that night they knew coffee, its growth, preparation for market, and last but not least, its treatment after it was in the pot. A heated discussion followed, for some started with cold water and some with hot. It is recorded that at this point the fumes of coffee pervaded the room and a delicious cup was served. This happy custom of Olla Podrida has quite disappeared, along with charades and other Victorian games. *Olla podrida* in Spain originally referred to a pot of mixed vegetables and meats all stewed together, and derives from the Latin *Olla*, meaning "pot," and *putridus*, meaning "rotten." Maybe the rotten part contributed to the abandonment of both the potpourri and the discussion.

So the family had in these years a happy time. The family also increased with great regularity, so that by 1878 there were six children in the house; the eldest boy was thirteen. The baby that was born in January was named Dorothy, or gift of God, apparently by Grandma Fearey in response to a note with pen-and-ink sketch of a great hand with a baby in its palm. The note reads: "Dear Grandma: What shall her name be? Affectionately your son, Edward Gay, Jan. 18, 8:00 P.M., 1878." It is evident that he knew how to get on with his mother-in-law; obviously he liked her.

That summer he took his two eldest sons Duncan and Ted on a wonderful trip: they walked to Albany. Two mementos of the trip remain. One is a group of stylized sketches, as if for a magazine or a newspaper story, with four vignettes on one page, most appealing, showing the camp with the tent and the cooking pot, the father pointing and the boys staring, with caption "The Hudson, Look"; the ride on the canal boat, and one boy sleeping. Another sketch shows the father cutting a very large watermelon as the boys look on with happy anticipation; and finally there is a pen-and-ink sketch of the party on the bank of the river, the father reading as he lies in a hammock, the boys beneath. The other item is a letter from Mattie to the travellers. It is dated August 22 and says, "Tomorrow is Birdie's birthday, so we thought of taking a little trip." Birdie was Vivien, and she was celebrating her tenth birthday. The boys were thirteen and twelve, and were surely stout fellows, as was their father, to walk the 150 miles to Albany. This trip is one of the few indications we have of the artist enjoying his children in any special way. In a letter about this time Martha writes him, "The weather has been hot and the little folk grow cross, and there is no one to peremptorily stop their howling." This brings to mind a proper Victorian paterfamilias.

Chapter VI

THE VOYAGE

> *One of the pleasantest things in the world is going a journey . . . The soul of a journey is liberty, perfect liberty, to think, feel, do just as one pleases.*
>
> —WILLIAM HAZLITT

The walk to Albany sealed the friendship with William J. Arkell, a wealthy manufacturer and newspaper publisher who lived in Canajoharie, for the walking party accepted his invitation to stop overnight with him. Willim J. Arkell and our artist became staunch friends, with a companionship that lasted through many years. Arkell was a patron of the arts and a collector, and it was during this visit that he developed his plan for a holiday trip for artists. Edward Gay was enlisted and most enthusiastic, so that he became the moving spirit in planning and organizing the trip, which actually came off in 1880. On this visit to Canajoharie, Edward Gay was given a commission for a large mural in the new Wagner Hotel at Canajoharie, completed the next year. Also, he was commissioned to do a landscape, "The Valley of the Mohawk," for William J. Arkell's brother Bartlett, who was president of the Beechnut Company—at that time entirely in bacon and meat packing. The picture was subsequently reproduced in the advertising of the Beechnut Company. It showed the broad valley of the Mohawk in summer with a puffing train in the middle distance. The scene for this picture was to be the view from the great Arkell house, and the artist and his wife were invited to visit in the house while making sketches for the large canvas. Arkell was a wealthy man and he and his wife lived in palatial style, but their meals proved inadequate for the young artist and his wife, so that each day they had to supplement the fare by buying sardines and crackers and milk which they ate in a secluded wood. These small picnics were happily recalled in after years.

Edward Gay was a member of the Artists' Fund Society, which was an organization of artists banded together to help the widow and family of any member who died (this was the purpose of the Fund, raised by exhibition and sale of pictures contributed each year by the members). Another objective was social, and this was pursued in the Annual Dinners, and in other gatherings. It was at these affairs that Edward Gay often was master of ceremonies; his ready wit and his store of stories, together with his sociability, all combined to make him the man wanted for these affairs. Thus it was appropriate that he should be selected by his friend Arkell to head the Committee on Arrangements for the "Voyage." In February the artist J. C. Nicoll writes: "Dear Gay: Arkell has fixed upon Monday 4 P.M. as the hour for the Powers dinner in my studio (at The Century, 100 East 15th Street)—hold yourself in readiness to attend." The four-o'clock time was set to allow time for formulating the plans for the trip. A. F. Bunner wrote on June 8th "Friend Gay—Hearing that you were the man on the Committee of the 'Artists Fund Voyage' . . . please let me know this programme . . . I thought of joining the party . . . at Albany or Troy . . . I want to be one of the 'Voyagers'." Daniel Huntington and M. De Forest Bolmer wrote regretting they could not make the journey.

This was indeed a marvelous voyage; in the end there was a party of some twenty-two artists, with William J. Arkell as host, and with several newspapermen. Publicity was a part of Mr. Arkell's plan, and he made sure that the newspapers got a running story. Edward Gay at age 43 was in charge.

The following is from the *Canajoharie Radii* of June 29, 1880:

The Artists' Excursion

The long talked of excursion of the members of the New York Artists' Fund Society, to Niagara Falls, via the Hudson River and Erie Canal, started at nine o'clock Monday morning.

The idea of this excursion originated with William J. Arkell of this place. Many New York artists are in the habit of visiting this section, and have usually become acquainted with Mr. Arkell. In several instances, intimacies of this kind have ripened into close friendships. This is notably the case with Edward Gay, an artist long and favorably known through the Mohawk Valley. Through Mr. Gay, Mr. Arkell some months ago extended an invitation to all the members of the Society to participate in the excursion, which has begun under such auspicious circumstances—and Mr. Gay is to be credited with doing a great share of the work, which always must fall on someone in organizing and conducting such an enterprise.

Nine o'clock Monday morning came, and at the same time a crowd of artists gathered on the pier, at the foot of the street; and as the *Chauncey Vibbard* came alongside, they stepped aboard and were mustered together while the roll was called by Mr. Gay. About eighteen answered to their names, including J. D. Barrow, A. T. Bricher, J. B. Bristol, A. F. Bunner, D. M. Carter, J. F. Cropsey, Percival De Luce, J. M. Falconer, H. Fuechsel, E. Gay, S. J. Guy, Thomas Hicks, A. C. Howland, G. H. McCord, J. C. Nicoll, Platt P. Ryder, A. Wordsworth Thompson, G. H. Yewell. Mr. Howard Lockwood, of New York City, a well-known publisher, and an intimate friend of Mr. Arkell, was also of the party.

Mr. Arkell was present, and untiring in his efforts to make the party comfortable. After the luggage was disposed of, all dispersed through the boat, as she drew out in the stream and sailed northward. J. G. Brown had bid the party good-by on the wharf, as he was prevented from going on account of a sick child. Mr. Arthur F. Tait was also at the wharf, but could not accompany the party, in consequence of a recent domestic bereavement.

It was a delightful day, and the sail was greatly enjoyed. All sat down to dinner in the saloon at 2 o'clock and an hour or more was consumed in disposing of a very good meal.

The Hudson River is, of course, very familiar to most of the party, and yet, with them, as with most people, it was difficult to refrain from expressions of delight as the *Vibbard* steamed through the Highlands. No sketch books, however, were produced—and in this respect this portion of the excursion is unrecorded.

At Tarrytown, Messrs. Alfred Jones and J. Williamson joined the party. At Newburgh the party was joined by D. M. Armstrong. Mr. Armstrong looked brown and hearty and received a cordial welcome from all. Mr. Arthur Parton met the excursionists later, at Canajoharie.

Albany was reached at 6:15, and carriages took the party to the Kenmore House, where all were soon comfortably located.

Immediately after dinner, all started for a drive. Washington Park was visited, and everyone was delighted with the charming manner in which it was laid out, the beautiful old trees and wide avenue drives. Soon after returning to the hotel most of the party retired.

Tuesday's programme began early, with a visit to the new Capitol building, right after breakfast. All seemed to agree that the building was very fine, but it was the apparently unanimous feeling that the decorations were far short of what was to be expected. One of the older members thought they would disgrace a Bowery Theatre. At nine o'clock all were on board the cars for Schenectady, at which place they arrived about 9:45. Carriages were in waiting, and Union College was visited. The Hon. Clarkson N. Potter met the party and escorted it to the Memorial Hall and afterwards to Jackson Garden. The latter place was very much enjoyed. All walked through it except Mr. Carter, who appreciated his mistake upon learning of the delightful drink of cool spring water obtained at the extreme end of the garden. Twenty minutes later and the party were carried to the steam yacht Jacob Amos, Jr. which had been in waiting for a day. Baggage was soon aboard, and amid the cheers of the citizens who lined the banks of the canal and thronged the bridge, the excursionists steamed away to the west. Shortly after starting, glasses were filled, and the health of "our noble host" was drank standing, and with cheers.

Everything was now fairly under way, sketch books were in every hand, and leaf after leaf was soon occupied with what will undoubtedly form the beginning of many valuable pictures.

The experience of riding through such a lovely country, on a "second-story river," as one of the company expressed himself, was a new one to almost every one of the party, and all took in eagerly every new view and the many quaint old houses and canal inns and grocery stores. The "natives" pleased everyone, and they in turn seemed to enjoy the music of Leppert's orchestra, which was on board. Frequently the boys and girls would run long distances to keep alongside. At every lock crowds collected and waved a welcome and adieu.

A sumptuous lunch was served in bow cabin during the afternoon, and was enjoyed greatly, especially the "washing down" process, which every man traveling by canal is supposed to adopt. This, at least, was impressed thoroughly on all.

At Yankee Hill Lock, just west of Amsterdam, stands an old country store. The boat was no sooner in the lock than all instantly jumped ashore, and in a moment at least sixteen artists were busily sketching the old house. Each one took a different view, and all worked so persistently that they failed to notice a carriage containing two ladies drive up. The ever-wakeful eye of the Chesterfieldian Gay rolled in the right direction, however, and knowing the ladies, he soon made all acquainted with Mrs. Greene and Miss Lathrop of Amsterdam. At the next lock the ladies came abroad the boat and the "stag" party was, for a time, broken up. At Empire Lock the ladies took to their carriage again, and with music and cheers adieus were said.

Canajoharie was sighted about six o'clock. For a mile or more the banks of the canal were dotted with groups of people, mostly ladies, who waved a welcome. Our artists responded vigorously, and at least a few were guilty of throwing kisses to pretty girls who had sense enough to be close by the "riverside." The party was divided between the Wagner and Nellis Houses, and after supper all spent a delightful evening at the residence of James Arkell.

On Wednesday morning the artists were early astir, and visited the picturesque falls of the Canajoharie Creek, which were reached by way of a romantic ravine, through which the stream flows, between rugged and precipitous cliffs, on its way to the Mohawk. The new Cemetery Park was also visited, and the artists were warm in their expressions of admiration for the taste which had planned it, and the judgment and skill with which the design had been carried out.

The sack factory of Messrs. Arkell & Smiths afforded the visitors an opportunity to contrast with the beauties of nature and art the marvels of mechanical contrivances, and the great results of human ingenuity in combination with the talent for the direction and organization, which builds up great business enterprises.

At about 11 A.M. the excursionists, with a large number of invited guests from Canajoharie and its vicinity, accompanied by Leppert's orchestra, which discoursed delightful music during the voyage, embarked again on the steam yacht, and were soon on their way to attend the reception and Rhode Island clam bake, tendered them by the Canajoharie Mining Company. Spraker's Basin, about three miles distant, was soon reached, and there carriages were in waiting to carry the party to the company's mines in Flat Creek, the scene of the reception.

Here in a secluded and romantic spot, preparations had been made for their entertainment with the most thoughtful and generous hospitality. The long tables, over-arched with green boughs, were spread with a lavish hand, and it soon appeared that a clam bake, in the Canajoharie sense, means a feast to tempt the most fastidious appetite. Mr. Howland, the president of the company, welcomed his guests with a few hearty words, and a combined attack was speedily made upon the choice edibles and drinkables with which the tables were laden.

The feast over, the artists dispersed in various directions, and were soon busily sketching the striking and picturesque features of the locality. After a day thus delightfully spent, the party returned to Canajoharie, the steam yacht bearing up the canal a pleasant and merry company, all arriving without accident at almost 6 P.M.

The artists then visited the old Frey house in Palatine Bridge, opposite Canajoharie, a stone structure erected in 1739, and from there repaired to the fine old mansion now occupied by S. L. Frey, the descendant of the original settler of that name. Here they inspected, with great interest, the historical collection which has been made with much industry and judgment by Mr. A. G. Richmond, cashier of the Canajoharie National Bank.

In the evening the party was entertained at the residence of Mr. W. J. Arkell, where, at the request of the guests, Mr. James Arkell favored them with a history of the origin, progress, perfection, and purposes of the Time Globe, an instrument of great ingenuity and interest, which is manufactured at Canajoharie by Juvet & Co.

The party will leave this morning on the steam yacht, for Utica, where they will arrive at about 6 P.M.

Naturally, on a trip like this there was no time for writing letters back home. Nevertheless, one is preserved; undated, it tells of the arrival at Rochester:

Dear Mattie, Here is Tuesday 6 A.M. and no word from you yet; but you told me not to worry about home. I am having such a glorious time that I cannot help wishing you could partake with me. Our day yesterday was but a repetition of the other days of pleasure. The country through which we passed is flat but exceedingly interesting. The day was hot but cloudy, giving infinite variety as the several passing showers swept over pastures, meadows and harvest fields, not to mention the rich fruit orchards.

The interest grows as we go on; here in Rochester as we entered the city all along the canal was lined by people young and old, the tops of the houses were packed, as well as the windows of the factories, cheering us and waving handkerchiefs and flags. The approach to Rochester is exceeding interesting, the canal winds around and in between some old and very picturesque houses, but the city itself is magnificent. Here more than any place since we left New York is it evident that the people are wealthy as well as energetic. Our party was met at the landing by D. P. Powers, a very wealthy gentleman who takes us off Arkell's hands during our stay, entertaining us at his own expense. Last night he gave us a grand reception at his art gallery (private). It is situated on the top floor of his block of building; the decoration and hangings of the gallery was something truly magnificent. Wealth was just lavished on the whole thing to make it as rich and sumptuous as possible. There we found hanging many of the finest pictures that we will know as having seen at Gonfils. Why, as I went around the gallery I could not help wondering that here were all the best pictures exhibited Gonfils the last ten years! This will give you some idea of the collection; there were many old masters but I did not pay much attention to them.

The reception was a grand affair. We stipulated for an informal one but the wealth and beauty of the place was there to meet us.

Today Mr. P. takes us out on the lake, down the bay, and also to see the Falls. He provides carriages at 9 o'clock and drives us through the city. We will dine at one o'clock, then get aboard his steam yacht.

I hope you will be able to read this—I am writing in a hurry to gather my boys for breakfast. The boys are very considerate and respectful to me, expressing their gratitude for this great pleasure. We stay here tonight, and will proceed on to Lockport at 7 A.M. tomorrow, reaching Niagara Wednesday morning, leaving N. Saturday at 8 o'clock for home.

Now come down to breakfast with me and I will introduce you to some of the notables who come to breakfast with us.

Kisses all around,

Your Edw. Gay

It was at the final dinner given at Niagara Falls on July 3rd, 1880 to the members of the "Artists Fund Excursion" party by Mr. William J. Arkell, that the following resolution was introduced and unanimously passed:

"*Resolved*: That the most cordial and hearty thanks of members of the Artists' Fund Excursion party are due to Mr. Edward Gay for the able and ready manner in which he has aided our amiable and generous host, Mr. William J. Arkell, in carrying out his hospitable intentions toward us. Mr. Gay has, in the most unselfish and thorough manner, assisted during the excursion, by every means in his power, in adding to the comfort and enjoyment of the party."[1]

There were other speeches and toasts at this parting dinner. "President Hicks toasted the ladies—wives and sweethearts, and Mr. Gay made a response in a touching, tender, and facetious vein in which he acknowledged that the glory of his inspiration came from his better half, Mrs. Gay, 'a glorious woman!'"[2]

---

1. *Utica Herald.*
2. Ibid.

Chapter VII

For golden friends I had . . .
—A. E. HOUSMAN

William J. Arkell, among his many enterprises, was a principal in the Arkell & Froehlich jewelry store in Canajoharie. It was through his friend Arkell that Edward Gay met another jeweler, the famous J. H. Johnston, who had a store at 150 Bowery on the corner of Broome Street in New York. He loaned the money to Thomas Fearey for purchase of the lot on 3rd Avenue immediately behind "434," and financed Edward Gay from time to time. Johnston was an art collector and in general a friend of artists and writers, and became a staunch friend. In writing of Walt Whitman, Henry Seidel Canby says, "Through the latter 1870's . . . the loneliness of Camden was broken by new friendships, such as a close and rewarding relationship with J. H. Johnston, a jeweler of New York and a personality. . . . With Johnston and his wife and children, whom he came to love, he stayed for a month at a time, and was able to renew happily many of his New York memories." We have no evidence that Edward Gay knew Whitman except for the copy of *Leaves of Grass* that he valued highly and which he presented to his grandson, telling him that he had bought it on the doorstep from Whitman himself. It is the first edition of 1855. On the flyleaf is written, as if with a paintbrush dipped in ink, Edward Gay's name and the date 1858. Stuck into the book was a page of manuscript in Whitman's handwriting, in which words and whole sentences were struck out and rewritten and then struck out and revised again. This sheet of manuscript and the *Leaves of Grass* are now owned by the library of the University of North Carolina.

If Edward Gay knew Whitman, and it surely seems likely he did, he knew that Walt, "an American," was writing directly to Edward Gay, who said "I am an American" with such pride. In "Song of Myself" Whitman wrote:

> Earth of shine and dark mottling the tide of the river!
> Earth of the limpid gray of clouds brighter and clearer for my sake!
> Far-swooping elbow'd earth—rich appleblossom'd earth!
> Smile, for your lover comes.

If Walt Whitman never saw Edward Gay's earth-landscapes, certainly we know that Edward Gay had read and reread this verse and that he painted his shine and dark mottling tide, his limpid clouds, and his rich apple-blossom'd earth in a manner the same as the gray poet saw them.

The close friendship the artist had with J. H. Johnston may be sensed in the two letters below, the first dated October 8, 1881.

> Dear Gay:
> How soon can I have that picture to square up the charge for the cameo pin?
> *Moreover*:
> Why haven't you been to see me since your return?
> Yrs. truly
> J. H. Johnston

And another letter dated April 30, 1887:
> My dear Mr. Gay:
> So you sat down and cried when you found you had drawn a $2500 prize! Well, I don't blame you, for I came very near crying myself just now when Mrs. Bruce Crane told me of it.

Left by the Tide, painted by Edward Gay, 1886.

> From the bottom of my heart, yes, way down to my heel tops, I congratulate you, and so will everyone who knows you, not only because you deserve it, but because you have a soul in you that has impelled you on to ultimate success.
>
> Your success makes me feel like going right into a Methodist camp meeting and shouting "Praise the Lord!" Extend my congratulations to your wife too, and believe me now and always,
> Very sincerely your friend,
J. H. Johnston

The prize of $2500 was awarded for the picture "Broad Acres" at the Prize Exhibition of the American Art Association in April 1887. The Secretary of the National Academy also wrote congratulations, as did many friends, notably A. G. Richmond, Cashier of the Canajoharie National Bank, whose sweet letter is worth quoting. It is dated May 2, 1887:

> My dear Gay: In response to your good news of the 29th ult., I do most heartily rejoice with you. I hope "Broad Acres" will multiply until there is a realty spread out before you for which you hold the deed.
>
> I have seen Mr. Arkell's people and they all rejoice with me at your success.
>
> I judge from the *World's* account that Gay was somewhat overcome, and needed the gentle assistance afforded by none but Mrs. Gay.
>
> I shall take special care to go to the Metropolitan when down, that I too may look upon "Broad Acres" . . .

This account, so chronological heretofore, has been allowed to get ahead of itself, but no matter. After the excursion by canal to Niagara, our artist settled down for a time of hard work. By the end of the year he had a hundred canvasses ready for a one-man show at Townsend and Evans at 107 E. 23rd Street in New York, February 24 to March 12, 1881. The terms of agreement were recited in a letter, "In accordance with your very proper wish we send you in the following lines our understanding of the agreement entered into between us. We will hang your pictures for sale in our Art Rooms from date (Feb. 24th) till March 12 inclusive and will sell them on the following terms—10% to us on the total proceeds from said sale; no picture to be sold less than the figure placed against it on your list with 25% added and no frames to be sold under 10% in advance of the list price. This we think covers the ground."

There was also a much larger show and sale held at Barker and Co., 47 & 49 Liberty Street on March 22 and 23, 1881. This comprised all the pictures not sold at the Townsend & Evans show and was an auction sale with a printed catalog listing 82 oil paintings and 18 water colors. George I. Banks was auctioneer. The catalog flyleaf says "Catalogue of Mr. Edward Gay's paintings, comprising a large variety of subjects, many of which have been painted directly from nature, and all FINISHED WORKS. Mr. Gay is about to sail for Europe, to remain an indefinite length of time; he therefore has decided to sell his entire collection WITHOUT RESERVE."

Also in this catalog are reprinted comments from the *New York Herald*, March 1, 1881, and also from the *New York Tribune*, March 6th, which were excellent pre-show publicity. Included also is the letter consigning the pictures:

                    Studio, Mt. Vernon, N. Y.
                    March 14, 1881

Messrs. Barker & Co.
Auctioneers, 47 & 49 Liberty St.

    Dear Sirs: I consign to you, today, my entire collection of pictures—oil and water colors. You will sell them by auction without reserve.

I feel assured by the success I have had in offering them at private sale during the past week that the public are sufficiently interested in my work to attend the sale and bid on my pictures.

Very truly yours,
EDWARD GAY

We have no record of the sales, but they must have been good since shortly thereafter Gay's friend William A. Seaver wrote him, "This is to certify, as emphatically as possible, that Edward Gay, Esquire and Artist, has paid me in grand cash the sum of one hundred and fifty dollars, in full liquidation of a note for that amount given in the year 1880, not long before he emitted himself from the country of excessive freedom to go abroad and 'pooh, pooh' at the rotten monarchies of Europe." Somehow our artist had raised the "grand cash" to pay debts and to finance a trip to Europe.

Chapter VIII

THE TRAVELS

The use of travelling is to regulate the imagination by reality, and instead of thinking how things may be, to see them as they are.
—Samuel Johnson

The 1881 trip to Europe was planned long ahead. The architect J. H. Magonigle, a fellow townsman, wrote a letter to Edwin Booth, in London. "Dear Ned," it said, "this will introduce to you my friend and fellow townsman Mr. Edward Gay, the artist, who is about to pay a visit to certain parts of Northern Europe in the interest of his art as well as for rest and recreation. As a member of the Academy, I know his name is not unfamiliar to you . . . ."

For this trip extensive and extended planning was indeed required. First there was the arrangement with Grandmother Fearey to take care of the family. This was quite a responsibility since there were seven children, ranging from Duncan at sixteen down to Dorothy aged three. The eldest girl was Vivien and she was thirteen. Aunt Lottie and the Irish maid of all work stayed in the house with the children, while Grandmother Fearey, with Grandfather Fearey, lived in the small house on Third Avenue, located just behind "434."

A postal card from Sharnbrook to Master Duncan Gay dated June 22, 1881 says, "Tell our charming Grandma Fearey that this place is one of the loveliest spots we have found yet. Your mama and I have made many sketches of the quaint old houses and streets. We go this afternoon to Oakly and Steventon. Do you look after everything and help Lottie . . . Kiss Dora for your Papa."

There have been stories of how wrong it was of the parents to leave the children, stories of the children being left without enough money, of their being fed by the neighbors. The travels, however, may be said to have been a necessary part of the business of the artist's career, and certainly Martha had to go with her husband: he came first. It is also possible that the hardship stories contain substantial exaggeration.

One of the stories tells us how short of money the travellers were. It seems that they concluded that, for the twelve-day Atlantic crossing, perhaps they could save a few dollars by wearing old clothes which they would discard on arrival, reserving their good clothes for use in London and for further travels. As there were no laundry facilities, they took along undergarments to wear and throw away, particularly the long woolens needed for the cold weather. So this was carefully worked out, and on arrival at London, steaming up the Thames, they had prepared a bundle of the old clothes which was duly heaved out of the porthole. The harbor police recovered the bundle from the water and presented it to them upon the wharf, saying they knew it had accidentally fallen from the ship. As there was nothing else for it, our travellers took the sodden bundle and piled into a hansom cab with their luggage. As the hansom crossed London Bridge, Edward Gay stopped the driver and chucked the bundle into the river again. But, alas, again the efficient police saw it fall and splash, and intercepted them, saying, "Aha! Getting rid of the baby, are ye?" Protests were of no avail, and they were taken into the police court and held until the "baby" was rescued and unwrapped in a most embarrassing manner. The police were relieved when they saw it was just soiled linen, and agreed to "drop it into the dust bin."

This was not a good way to arrive in London, but their hansom took them on along the Embankment and into Norfolk Street where, at No. 26, was Bumyard's Hotel, a place of family chambers with a boardinghouse-style dining room.

Norfolk Street runs from the Strand rather steeply downhill to the Embankment; it was called Norfolk Street because in this street were two of the town houses of the Duke of Norfolk. These houses may be seen today. The numbering has been changed, but we can be fairly certain that the great five-story house on the corner of Norfolk Street and the Embankment was Bumyard's Hotel: it is impressive today, with its doors with stained-glass surrounds, its noble stairway surmounted by a stained-glass lantern skylight. A lift has been installed, and the building is today mainly solicitors' offices. An inquiry at one of these brought out an old gentleman who might well recall 1881; but he said no, his firm had been there but a few years, "only since 1907." But he did know that at one time there were altogether chambers there.

Martha tells of this trip in her 1921 account:

> In 1883 we sailed for a trip abroad—England, with perhaps a trip to Paris, Holland and Norway. It was one of those times when Fenian Ireland takes the bit in teeth and England had accused the United States of supplying arms to the Fenians. Passengers had been searched on English ships. "Do not mention that I am Irish," Edward Gay had warned us. It might be a study in Americanization—the attitude of these two toward their native land. There was nothing in him to suggest the Irishman (tall, gaunt, with gray eyes in his pallid face). He often had been accosted in crowds as "Uncle Sam," but his speech had a brogue, a delightful brogue to Martha's ear. They found lodgings in London where, at the breakfast table, he amused himself and the English lodgers with stories of a humor so subtle any one might have known him for an Irishman—but not they. One morning after they had left the breakfast table, she heard the other guests say, "Typical Americans!" Could anyone be more American than she, born in Bedford, right among them, and Edward Gay, an Irishman to the

marrow? Could anything be more sharp than the Englishman? All day she felt enraged that she had been, so to speak, sworn to silence. But for this, what a happy day they had! Then in the evening, returning across London Bridge, they passed an old Irishwoman selling from a basket of oranges. "Oh, buy me an orange, Edward!" As he stooped to pay her he remarked, "You are a long way from Tipperary, Mother." "Not a bit farther than you are from Mullingar, my son!" Martha bubbled with joy at the encounter.

Afterward, nothing of that London day remained in Martha's memory but the old woman selling oranges. Yet, they had been all day in the National Gallery standing most of the time before the Constable canvasses, which seemed to the artist the finest observation of nature. He was to do it afterward, to paint just such sweeping clouds touched with light. To devote his brush to the simple beauty of green fields or growing grain until those who looked at the canvas would seem to themselves to be walking the little wandering path through remembered fields. This gamut of color, cool, clear green and blue and delicate prismatic gray, wiped from his mind all the harsh insults of his German study. He was to see color under fair noonday skies with the consummate color of day, as in that canvas painted in immemorial gray, looking toward the pool, where lay the faint blue of the zenith of his dreaming; or that other canvas "After the Rain," where the gray clouds fly from the face of the sun and the green fields are shattered rainbows; or that smaller canvas, "Ripening Grain," where the green stems grow subtly into cadmium under the grayest of skies. All these were the scheme of color in which Constable had brought landscape painting to the foremost rank in the history of the art, and which the Barbizon School was to recognize.

Perhaps among the Barbizons it was Lambrint to

whom Edward Gay's work was most closely allied. The gentle lines of the Frenchman's landscape were so carefully studied but painted with an easy awareness. Perhaps no critic has written of this in Edward Gay pictures, but his sense of line did not fail the line of horizon, the sweeping directness of trees where the branches bowed under the prevailing winds or the unerring perspective of the little humble path that led away and away with the footsteps of the generations—all these seemed to give to the canvas a living beauty. You also walked that pleasant path and the sense gave to his canvas movement in the way the moderns use the word. He is alive, a veteran (the Academicians call him that today) among those moderns, and now at 84 years he is painting with as swift a brush.

The 1881 trip seems unhurried. There was a happy stay in London, with pleasant times with their old Albany friend George H. Boughton. Boughton had been born in England, but like Edward Gay had been brought to Albany when a boy. He studied art in Albany and became a competent painter; he went to live in London, gained a reputation as a portrait painter, and was made a member of the Royal Academy.

In the March 1883 issue of *Art Amateur*, an article on Boughton by Frederick W. White tells of Boughton's youth in Albany with his six fellow artists: "One was a wheelwright, another a carpenter, a third a carriage painter, a fourth a bartender, a fifth a doctor's office-lad, and the sixth an unsuccessful furrier's apprentice. Not one of them had any acquaintance with the purple and fine linen of life. But they could paint a little, or thought they could, and he who was least proficient in the art they loved was taught by his advanced fellows . . . . It is amazing that each one of that Albany group has made for himself a name. The art world knows them today as E. D. Palmer, the sculptor, James M.

Hart, Lamont Thompson, Edward Gay, William Hart and George H. Boughton."

While this quotation contains much literary license, especially the grouping the older men with the younger, it does give interesting confirmation to the story that Edward Gay was employed as a bartender.

At the time of this visit to London, Boughton lived at West House, Campden Hill Road, W., which Martha says was part of the wall of the London waterworks; and there the Gays were invited to a "family lunch at half past one sharp." This was a happy reunion, for Boughton dropped his plans for the summer and went to Paris with the Gays.

Martha insisted that she must return to her birthplace in Bedfordshire, so they went to Steventon (there is a sketch dated 1881 and titled "Stevington"), and from Sharnbrook they sent the card to the sixteen-year-old Duncan. They also went to Brighton, surprisingly enough, as we know from a sketch with date 1881. Then came a visit to Ireland; four pen-and-ink sketches have been preserved, signed and titled: "Quarry Bog, Westmeath"; "Gateway Knockdrin Castle"; "Mullingar on the Brosna"; and "Home of Kate Kearney."

Martha says:

> On that little run to Paris, George Boughton left his London studio, which he had built as part of the Wall of the London Water Works, and went with us to get a glimpse of the Spring Salon. I remember when the gate clicked at my entry he remarked, "You are Number 10,000, Mrs. Gay." Oh, the Paris Salon of the Eighties and the canvasses that held us, we young Americans! That old painter, Claude Monet—was he young then? "You must see this!" George Boughton said. This was a pink and purple canvas, a huntsman with the game at his feet on the hillside, a canvas of colors to which new eyes must be readjusted. We were to see twelve canvasses of the Cathedral at Rome under the varying light

and shade of the hours of a day. Looking at them one became slowly aware of what the eye might see closely, slowly and vaguely aware of what it was missing and aware too of that great mistress of art who invited us into her wide domain. Corot was there. Corot, that Greek. It had not been many years before that, walking up Fifth Avenue in New York, she had turned into Knoedler's (or was it in Barker's Old Gallery?) and there hung a canvas by a new name—Corot—and grouped around it those old men, familiar in every gallery, to pass criticism on this painter whom Frenchmen acclaimed. Presently there was room for her. How simple, how straightforward! What pearly light held the scene—the Village Church, the brook at the foot of the hill, the clump of trees, all as in an alembic of light. That was but a small canvas, but here was this great "Dancing of the Nymphs," nature at one with the Gods. The ancient Gods who fret not, nor fume. It is well that Americans learned so swiftly to love Corot. He is of their kind, young as the Greek was in the growth of the world.

There was one painter, Flamany, before whose canvas they stood for long—or did they stand? Rather, they seemed to themselves to walk in these green fields. It was such work as this that Edward Gay aspired to do; by some glamour of color and line to take the spectator into the scene. She thought of his canvas "Washed by the Sea," where air and shore shone crystal-clear clean from the bath of the sea and you breathed the sweet salt air.

But Boughton would have them go to the Musée Cluny to view a wonder of tapestries. He was himself adept at stitches, knowing web and woof and all the mysteries of threads, perhaps as Helen of Troy knew it when she sang into her weaving all tales of gods and men. What haste they were in! She just recalls that

Boughton stopped them as they were to mount the ancient staircase to observe the newel post of such workmanship. You remember that lovely large upper gallery at Cluny, all tapestried about between the wide clear glass windows in scenes from which the figures—men and women from other days—seemed to beckon you into the gardens in which they belonged? How far one travels being led by art!

It was not London, nor even Paris, that called the artist Edward Gay away from America but, and how unsophisticated it seems, Norway: the blue of its soundless fjords, the green of those valleys and the great cumulus clouds that rise newborn above the crags, the mountains of the sky.

April roses, freshly picked cool in the night air, in which they have gathered richness, lie in my lap as I write. Petal on petal of pink to the outer sweet fold, just so lay the little Norwegian town of Molde, its gray homes over-run with Marchal Neil roses of the softest bloom. We had sailed up the Sogne Fjord from Bergen on the Hardanger to this northernmost city of roses. Above the roses was that blue sky with moving clouds and before us stretched the green of fields to the water's edge. It was never pictures that moved Edward Gay to paint, but nature itself. When in the school at Karlsruhe he had seen the canvasses of the Norwegian Gude and he had felt, "I must see those scenes. Could I but see that northern color I would paint it!" And we were here. Constable, Lamont and Corot grew dim in memory, and he painted day and night in those northern latitudes with a wild joy that he looked on the secret of color until his tired eyes refused to see. A large canvas hangs in the drawing room of a Southern home: its title, "Hardanger Fjord," where the fjord is unplumbed and the glacier is on the mountain. He was to be caught and tangled in these romantic subjects, yet on his return to

America, he painted and sold and found himself at ease in his finances. There hangs a prize picture of these Norwegian fjords in a gallery at Minneapolis. When at length Norway was far behind he found color unweighted by his subject. He returned to the fields as a child gathers daisies. Nothing could be more simple than "The Road to Scarsdale" or "Broad Acres" (the latter hangs in the Metropolitan Museum in New York—the Board Room), or perhaps "Gathering Leaves," an autumn scene.

As Martha realized at the time, Norway was of great importance in the life of Edward Gay as an artist. He seems to have savored it with immediate enthusiasm. They went first to Bergen, and there could be no happier introduction to Norway. In July the climate is ideal; always the fjords and craggy mountains tie the land to the sea.

Bergen has two heroes, each a musician, and it happened that Edward Gay knew them both. The great violinist Ole Bull had been on concert tours to New York, where Edward Gay had met him. He urged Gay to go to Norway, gave him a letter to Edvard Grieg, and said he must go to Bergen and see him.

Apparently the artist and Grieg got on at once and became firm friends. The diminutive Grieg and our tall, slender Edward Gay made a strange pair. Grieg invited him to go fishing with him in the fjord below his house and he agreed readily, saying that he was no fisherman but that he'd like to sit in the stern of the boat and paddle while Grieg sat in front and cast his line.

All was quiet and calm as they paddled slowly over the clear water. It was a time of quietness, so there was no talk. Grieg fished, while our artist studied the scene of the fjord and the mountains and the limpid water. Then Grieg made an especially vigorous cast of his line, and as he did so a slip of paper fell from his pocket. It floated beside the boat back to Edward Gay, who reached down and retrieved it. He was about to give it back to Grieg when he saw that pencilled on the paper were a few bars of music, obviously a composition of the great musician. The artist could read music, having learned in boyhood when he was a choirboy. Quickly he memorized the short theme, and putting the bit of paper into his own pocket, he whistled the phrase. He whistled it again, more loudly.

Grieg wheeled on his seat and growled, "Where'd you get that?"

Gay answered, "Oh, it's just something that came to me."

It was while at the little town of Molde in Norway, where they stayed some weeks, that the news came to them of the shooting of President Garfield. This was on July 2, 1881; and one of Martha's tales had them returning from a sketching trip and finding it was after midnight when they got back to their lodgings, the midnight sun shining bravely. Then the news in a note on the pillow plunged them into blackest gloom: to think that an assassination could happen again in America! Poor Garfield lingered on and did not die until September, long after Edward Gay's safe return home.

In Paris in April was held the Sixth Group Show of the Impressionists, with thirteen participants. The state had returned control of the Salon to the Academy, and at the Salon that year were two Renoir portraits of *Mlle S.* (Samarz) and the double portrait of *Cohen-d'Anvers;* Manet had two paintings accepted, while Cézanne was again rejected; Puvis de Chavannes' *Poor Fisherman* was there, and it so impressed Seurat that he made a sketch copy of it. "Monet never sends anything to the Salon," says John Rewald, writing of the 1881 Salon, so perhaps it was somewhere else that Martha saw the Monets she mentions.

Our travellers had a room high up, with a balustrade, in the Rue Tronchet. The Rue Tronchet is a short street behind the Madeliene. It is a most convenient location. They took the little bateau-mouche down to Saint-Cloud, where Edward Gay made a small picture of the Seine. And yet, for some reason, Martha did not enjoy Paris. Two years later, when Edward Gay went back to Paris, she writes, "Enjoy Paris as I did not." We must conclude that she had a bad cold, or worse, since Martha ordinarily enjoyed life more than most people.

It should be noted that in 1881 Edward and Martha were much interested in the political scene in England. Gladstone was supporting the Irish Land Reform Act, carried in Parliament while the Gays were in London. They wrote ahead in order to get permits for admission to the House of Commons. A cordial reply was received from Chas. S. Parnell, P.H.C. This was Charles Stewart Parnell, the great Irish patriot who was imprisoned later in the same year. There was a similar note from John Daly.

We may be sure that this 1881 trip was very stimulating. As Martha says, on his return home Edward Gay plunged into work with renewed vigor and enthusiasm, and with success too, since Martha records that "he painted and sold and found himself at length somewhat at ease in his finances." The sketches made in Norway were the basis for his winter work in his studio, while as soon as warm weather came he went back to his outdoor painting of salt marshes and fields.

The year 1882 was one of busy and successful work, as well as busy associations with his friends of the art world in New York. We have noted earlier that in March of this year he was chairman of a large exhibition of paintings given by some seventy artists for the benefit of the Irish Famine Fund. You may be sure that many of these artists were friends of Edward Gay.

In March of 1883 another baby arrived at "434." It was a boy and he was named George Inness, after the friend who was perhaps the most prestigious of contemporary American landscape painters.

In May of 1883 Edward Gay went off to Europe again,

this time without Martha as she had to stay with the new baby. He was accompanied by his friend and fellow townsman Joseph S. Wood. Mr. Wood was the superintendent of the school and was also editor of *The Chronicle*. The records of this trip are few, but we do know that they went in early May and on the same ship, the "Queen" on which Edward and Martha had crossed two years earlier. They also went to stay at Bumyard's Hotel in Norfolk Street, and the purpose of the trip for Edward Gay was undoubtedly to see pictures. On May 6th Martha writes to him of the beauties of spring in Westchester, concluding, "But you will be saying 'who cares?', for as you read it is pictures whose color, subtler than nature because penetrated with intellect, entrances you."

The travellers went on to Paris where they stayed at the Hotel Binda. While they were there a letter came from Martha telling how "there came a catalogue of the Charleston Exhibition with your name and picture." This began Edward Gay's connection with South Carolina, which was to become more important a few years later. Martha was a good letter-writer, and her husband knew it and preserved a number of her letters. She was writing art criticism pieces for the *Albany Evening Journal*, and she said to Edward, "Be sure and bring illustrated catalogues for me, and keep the beautiful pictures in mind for me."

The 1883 trip was a quick trip for those days. The two travellers were away eight weeks, and they probably needed almost half the time for the ocean crossings. They returned via Dublin and Cork, sailing from Queenstown. Writing to Martha from Cork on June 12th, 1883, Edward says in a letter which is interesting enough to be quoted in its entirety:

> Dear Mattie: We reached here last night at 8 o'clock and, to think of it, just as we crossed the bridge up started the "Bells of Shannon" as if to welcome us. We left Dublin in the morning and slowly went along to Cork, passing through Tipperary, Queens County, and

ever so many bogs. The day was glorious, so I need not say we thorougly enjoyed it.

We had several hours to see the sights in Dublin and we made the most of them—went to Phoenix Park and took a good look at Kilsnaham, not knowing but perhaps before we were ready to start they would put us in for safekeeping.

They let us off, tho; I suppose Mr. W. kept me within bounds; he is awfully afraid I will do something awful and keeps correcting me at all times, which is too much for a saint to bear, but we let him have his sweet way and I have mine. We will look around here tonight and tomorrow morning take the boat down the river to Queenstown.

But today we went to Blarney Castle, kissed the veritable stone, so now we are ready to go home and use our power over you all. The walk was four miles, the road winding through the most delightful fields imaginable—no sign of poverty or trouble, beautiful farms and houses all the way. Get Dana's collection of poems and read Lottie Sheil's "Groves of Blarney," for it is quite accurate and to the point.

We called on the old man you and I met at Bumyards from Shannon Church—you recollect him. He had his house full of old stuff, books and other trash. Very soon he remembered me and treated us kindly and wanted to be remembered to you surely, for "you were a remarkably bright and likely woman." We promised.

We will probably go to Killarney tomorrow and on Thursday sail for home. Mr. W. calls me to supper now; I must go, for if I keep him waiting he will be furious! Coming!

We have just been out to see the city by evening light and it is most surprising. It is really a beautiful city, so many imposing churches and public buildings.

Both sides of the river have embankments like the Thames, and it must have been done years ago.

The very old is exceedingly picturesque. Two branches of the river meet just in the city and the shipping comes up to the bridge like in London. But I must let it go till I come home now.

We leave here at 9 A.M. for Queenstown. We go down the river so that we may see the scenery. The evidence of prosperity here is cheering.

We are counting the pennies now as we are almost broken, but we will get to Queenstown as that only costs one shilling, then the steamer and home!

Lots of love to all,
                                        Your Edward Gay

Of all the people in the world Edward Gay was the man who least of all needed to kiss the Blarney Stone. Or it may be that the "veritable stone" gave him the great "power" that he "used over us all." Blarney connotes smooth, wheedling talk, perhaps cajoling talk, and sometimes flattery. It is the "gift of gab," frequently associated with insincere coaxing or beguiling with a selfish objective. In the Irish the beguiling was emphasized. Of course, in the Irish nature, the selfish object was missing, and insincerity was unknown.

In writing of Blarney Castle, Robert Gibbings says, "that stream (the Shournagh) flows beside a village as famous as the city of Carthage, Pompeii or Thebes. What city, town, or village in the world has given its name as noun and verb to the English or any other language? Only one; the village of Blarney." To which one may say, what about Buncombe?

Chapter IX

*This world is a difficult world,
indeed,
And people are hard to suit,
And the man who plays on the
violin
Is a bore to the man with a
flute.*
—WALTER LEARNED

Edward Gay was much beloved by his many friends. He was hail fellow well met, he was gay, and he was a great storyteller. Yet he was also distrusted by the conservatives of the National Academy of Design, so that for year after year, despite his outstanding successes, he was refused the accolade of full membership as National Academician. At the age of thirty-two he had been made Associate; he did not get the full N.A. until he was seventy, and it would not be less than the truth to record that he suffered acute disappointment in most of the years between. He was truly beloved and greatly aided by his wife Martha, who worshipped him. She gave him ten children, children that he appeared not to want and not to love. He did little for them; they feared him and respected him, but of them all only a few loved him.

Duncan, the eldest son, went to work at age fourteen to get money to help feed the family; at sixteen the second son, Ted, was sent to Albany to work in the shoe factory of Martha's father. Some of the children, especially Duncan, Vivien and Patty, had obvious inherited talent in art, but their father refused to teach them and he would never encourage them.

Edward Gay and Martha were personalities so dominant that they overshadowed the children and gave them little opportunity and little attention. While the children truly loved Martha they resented their father's demands upon her, that she must stay with him and read to him as he worked. Yet we would do a grave injustice to Edward Gay if we did not recall some of the times that he was a happy parent who did much for his children. These instances mostly come from his younger years, as in the story of the wonderful walk to Albany with the two boys. There is also the touching story of how at the age of five Dorothy was taken by her father to pose for a friend, who was doing a portrait of a mother and child. Dorothy sat in for the child, and became very tired. Her father saw she was tired and took her into St. Patrick's, saying, "Just say a little prayer and you will find you are not tired." Another story has to do with Helen when she was ten years old. Martha was away on a trip that seemed to Edward Gay to last too long. He had Helen dress up in a dress and a big hat borrowed from their friend Miss Levi, the opera singer. He had the photographer come, stood Helen upon a box, and he stood beside her. She cut her eyes at him in a most flirtatious way, while he smiled at her. He sent the photograph to Martha with a short and pointed note, "You'd best come home!"

Edward Gay was little interested in having his children go to school, to say nothing of college. Yet, as we have seen, he was indeed proud when his eldest daughter Vivien won a scholarship to study architecture at Cornell. He sold a piece of land to get money to help her.

It is hard to see how Martha found time to do all she did, yet at an early time in her marriage she began regular visits to the galleries and the show-rooms, and on returning home she wrote her criticism and comment. Some years passed before her writing was accepted by a newspaper, but eventually Edward's friend William J. Arkell, publisher of the *Albany Evening Journal*, persuaded his Editor Beers to make an arrangement with her for regular pieces. These pieces (1883-1895) were titled *"Art in New York"* and they were signed "M.F.G." and "Lady Gay." One, dated January 1885, is quoted:

> You remember that first picture that made you happy, and now how crude and poor it seems in the light of this better picture that makes you glad today. By and by perhaps this may seem thin and ineffective when you look back at it from some great canvas that wholly fills your imagination until almost unwittingly you have grown to the intellectual level of the master, up successive steps of delight.

Albany, of course, was home for Martha, more than for Edward Gay. She adverts to their early years there in her 1921 story, of which the following is the final quotation, bringing us to the end of it:

> In Albany also at that early day in the 60's, Homer D. Martin was beginning to paint the banks of the Hudson, the little lighthouse at Cedar Hill—ugly things, no sense of scene to them, but to be looked at perhaps for the things they were not. Winter after a fall season in the North woods he fairly revelled in the red and yellow of autumn foliage. They were all painting it: Sonntag, McEntire and Casilear, but out of this time Homer Martin's art was to emerge into such a canvas as "The Dunes of Lake Ontario"—wind-swept art in its brilliant sublime moment. Edward Gay was perhaps to do nothing as profound as this work.
> In this work of Homer Martin, the scene was fading and the movement of light and air was as in the canvasses "Waste Land" and "Mother Earth." It was a good deal to ask of an American public to look at a hay rick painted by Monet; nothing but a hay rick, and then to

find in this painting the glory of the sun. Yet New York City at last was ready for impressionism, and Durand-Reuel made no idle venture when he opened galleries on Fifth Avenue for the exhibition of Monet, Sisley, Pagano and all their French school. With them was one American woman, Mary Cassatt. The National Academy of Design frowned on them, to be sure, but it is the prerogative of an academy to be conservative! None of the Academy's exhibitions showed the influence of impressionism, yet interest in this new method, touch by touch of unmixed pigments upon the canvas, cleaned up the pallette of many a painter! More than that, the new work drew the attention of the picture-loving public to the relation of the observer's eye to the work of the artist. Fresh interest throbbed through the galleries.

There were no college men in Mount Vernon and all of them Americans in the process of making. Edward Gay, the artist, even more than his fellow citizens got his education outside of the schools. Mrs. Gay read aloud while the artist painted, beginning with Ruskin and Taine through all the German Romanticists—after the reading of Carlyle. Then a long stretch of philosophy —Swedenborg, then Kant—whose difficulties sent them back into art again. It was Aristotle and at length Plato, where Edward Gay rested as one taking to the road again. All this reading had been with the profoundest attention while the silent brush moved unhesitatingly from canvas to palette, and the pictures grew in those winter hours.

In writing for the papers Martha was pretty careful to resist the temptation, strong though it must have been, to praise her husband's work. There is but one instance of this, in the December 2, 1885 issue of the *Albany Evening Journal*, when she wrote of the Fall Exhibition of the National Academy of Design:

A Progressive Painting

    The place of honor in the center of South Room is occupied by Mr. Edward Gay's "Washed by the Sea." An inlet of the Sound, its muddy bottom left bare by the outgoing tide; great sweeps of salt meadow and boats updrawn leaving wonderful reflections in the liquid mud, and a strong wide sky, full of light and air. The scene is so simple that it strikes you as bold. Mr. George Inness said of the picture in his incisive way, "Why, it is the most progressive canvas yet painted in America." And perhaps it is because of this, that almost without a scene he has suggested the great spaces of air and light that brood over the gleaming tide.

Having read Martha's comment we should now see the letter that George Inness wrote to Edward Gay about the picture. Although caviling and condescending, it is real praise. Inness was at the height of his fame, and praise from him meant much; the letter also raised false hope that the N.A. award would finally be won.

    Dated Nov. 16, 1885, it says:
    My dear Gay:
        I had intended to write you some days since about your splendid success in the last picture at the Academy but I have been very busy and with my general disinclination to write letters I did not fulfill that intention.
    But I will express to you my belief that your picture "Washed by the Sea" is the finest piece of nature in tone and colour that has ever been on our walls. To my knowledge nothing of local force is shirked and the tone is nature's. The gradation leaves nothing to be asked for and the greater part of the picture is magnificently rendered. The lower sky is perfect but the upper clouds might be improved and the blue although fine in quality

needs to be reduced with darker tone leaving the darkest spots as they are. The water line does not appear quite level owing to the dropping of its tone at the left. There are a few things on the right hand of the picture which can easily be benefitted with a few touches.

There was at first some opposition to my opinion, but after I had got it hung in its present place there was general agreement that I was about right. In haste,

Yours truly,
George Inness

The success of "Washed by the Sea" encouraged Edward Gay to do a number of pictures of the shining mud of the salt meadows of Long Island Sound. In 1886 he did a large canvas titled "Left by the Tide," of the same great sweep of salt meadows, with the bright sky reflected in the shine of the mud flats, and with a sailboat left aground. The salt air is truly there. Walter Kerr in his *Decline of Pleasure* says: ". . . there is a substructure in painting, in music, in any experience of the beautiful which whispers to us that it *is* beautiful and not merely handsomely assembled. However this intimated substructure may be defined—whether one wishes to say that it has been truly overheard from nature or that it is a lucky accident come to spontaneous combustion in an artist's brain, brawn and bowels—it is the penetrating whisper upon which our truly hearing the artist depends, the 'inscape' that makes the landscape luminous. Indeed, it is not only a conviction that this interior coherence exists that keeps the artist thrashing at his materials long after he has mastered the trick of duplicating resemblances, it is the command of this hidden coherence that initially sets him to work. The restlessness of the artist comes from his impatience with mere appearances."

Similarly, Joseph Conrad in the preface to *The Nigger of the Narcissus* says, "To arrest, for the space of a breath, the hands busy about the work of the earth, and compel men entranced by the sight of distant goals to glance for a moment at the surrounding vision of form and color, sunshine and shadows; to make them pause for a look, for a sigh, for a smile—such is the aim, difficult and evanescent," of the artist.

Martha always stressed the intellectual quality of art; even in a newsy letter she says, "It is pictures whose color, subtler than nature because penetrated with intellect, entrances you." Edward Gay was thoughtful and intellectual, if you will, but his thoughtfulness and his intellectuality did not show in his painting except as we recognize that inner coherence that tells us it *is* beautiful.

Chapter X

THE PRODUCTIVE YEARS; 1884-1909

> *The wild vicissitudes of taste . . .
> For we that live to please must
> please to live.*
> —SAMUEL JOHNSON

Writing in 1884 to his old friend E. D. Palmer, the sculptor, Edward Gay enclosed a check for fifty dollars in part payment of an old debt and said he was sending a picture that he hoped would settle the balance outstanding. Palmer wrote his acceptance, dated May 18, 1884.

My dear Gay,

Your esteeemed favor of the 13th, enclosing your check for fifty dollars, was received in due time, and deserved an early reply, for it is so like your own self—manly, truthful and frank.

Of course, I will take the picture and gladly too, for I have only one of your works, that is a very early effort representing Tea Island, Lake George, painted I think during your first part summer at the lake. The picture is quite small. I have three or four of Boughtons, three of J. M. Hart, two of William Hart, and two of Homer Martin; now I shall have two of Gay's.

It seems quite curious that I see "Reapers' Lane" with the "Head of Innocence" that I made. You and Church own the entire lot. For the one Church had he gave me the "Twilight" I value so highly and for which I have refused $1400. Soon I suppose someone will come along and try to buy my Gay. Well, we'll see how successful he will be.

Enclosed find your note which I have kept carefully all these years.

Please bear our kindest regards to Mrs. Gay, and believe me your friend.

E. D. Palmer

The "Head of Innocence" was a life-sized oval marble bas-relief, in a mahogany frame supported at a sloping angle by a mahogany pedestal. It represented the head of a young girl. It was an appealing Victorian fixture in the front parlor at Mount Vernon for many years.

Edward Gay was painting and showing; he was awarded a medal at the New Orleans Exposition in 1885 and also at the Midwinter Exhibition in San Francisco. He was showing water colors, too. Martha wrote for the *Albany Evening Journal* of Nov. 17, 1885 of the Water Color Exhibition:

Springtime in the City, by C. Hassam, has an outdoor quality pleasant to see. A new name, this, but indeed there are so many new names that it gives one a little pang to be so long coming to the old remembered touch of Mr. Smillie and Van Etten and Cropsey and Nicoll. Just now the law of supply and demand is broken in upon by this army of student painters, each one questioning the future after fame, and the old warning is for each one of them, "many are called, but few are chosen."

Of course, Martha was right. There was a lot of competition coming along, and Childe Hassam along with other new names was to out-distance many of the older men. Yet Edward Gay did make a living, and quite a good and happy life he had. He worked hard, and he sold pictures. He somehow continued to get favorable comment in the newspapers. In the *New York Daily Tribune* of December 13, 1885, in a column entitled "City Chat and Comment—What

Men Are Talking About When They Get Together," the following note appears:

> Edward Gay, the artist, lives quietly at Mount Vernon. He is a tall and lean-faced man, whose leanness is made more marked by a long goatee and drooping mustache. He wears a soft felt hat, which gives him a Western air, though he is a New Yorker. He told me yesterday a joke about himself that he relished highly. He has a boy of seven or eight years and took the youngster to the Academy Exhibition. The little fellow had heard the talk at home about the criticism, and when he reached the Academy he insisted on being led at once to the place where his father's picture hung. He looked at it intently with the eye of a connoisseur, cocking his head gravely on one side and then on the other. Then his eyes swept around the room and rested on other paintings. "They say it is the best picture here," he finally commented. "Humph, I don't think so!"

This is a good illustration of the deft hand of the artist in his ability to invent something that would appeal to the reporter who needed to fill his column. His son Will was eleven at the time, and while he might have been taken to the Academy, somehow one is inclined to doubt it.

Edward Gay had a lively correspondence with fellow artists partly to feel the market and partly keeping in touch at a time when letters were a more important means of contact than they are today. The following letter from A. H. Wyant, dated at Stratford, Aug. 17, 1886, is obviously in response to an inquiry:

Mr. Gay
Dear Sir—
  'An Irish Landscape' has $1,000 for a price. The one called 'A Gray Day' has $300 fixed upon it.
                              I am truly yours,
                              A. H. Wyant

There are few records of the prices that Edward Gay received for his pictures until he made a happy arrangement with William Macbeth in the early 1890's. This excellent and progressive dealer became a good friend, and some of the artist's correspondence with him has been preserved. In general it was the practice for the artist, guided by the dealer at whose gallery his paintings would be shown, to name a sale price and a "net" price to the artist. The net price was the least the artist would take; if a sale was made at a higher price than specified by the artist, the dealer was entitled to pocket the extra commission, though it was usual for him to make an upward adjustment of the price to the painter.

Some prices recorded:
  Dec. 1897—*Harvest Field* $150 net
  Oct. 1899—Pictures at Worcester, Mass. A letter from the artist suggests reducing the price from $250 to $135 net "in order to sell."
  Nov. 1900—*The Springtime* $250 net to me $150
              Grainfield Harvesting $200 net $125
  Apr. 1903—*Path Homeward* $250 net $150
  May 1903—*Hillside in Spring* $150 net to me $75

In February 1903 Macbeth sold a Lillian M. Genthe *Landscape* for $400 and her *Head of Young Woman* for $200. The net to the artist was probably half the sale price. In May 1908 Macbeth sold Arthur B. Davies' *Spring's Recall* for $250.

In those days of no inflation and no income taxes a hundred dollars was an excellent and a substantial sum, and a good living for a family was thought to be possible with an income of four to six thousand dollars. Edward Gay's pictures, in the twenty-five years from 1884 to 1909, probably sold for an average price of $150 net to him, so that for a total income of $6000 per year he would have had to sell forty pictures. This comes to more than three pictures a month, and it meant working hard, painting in every daylight hour. There was no usable artificial light: Edward Gay tried to paint by the harsh glare of a gas mantle, but quickly found it distorted colors. He was assiduous and industrious, but there is never any indication of hardship. He loved his work and could be happy only when productive.

We have already noted that in 1887 Edward Gay won a prize of $2500 for *Broad Acres*. The picture was bought "by a group of gentlemen" and presented to the Metropolitan Museum of Art, probably upon the instigation of Gay's great friends J. H. Johnston and William J. Arkell. This was a very large canvas, and while it was hung for some years among contemporary American paintings, it was afterwards put into the Board Room, where it practically covered one wall. Neither this picture nor any other picture of Edward Gay's was included in the Metropolitan's new American Painting Wing which opened in 1971. The $2500 prize and the sale of the picture did wonders, you may be sure, for the budget at "434"; and it was grand publicity that surely helped to sell other pictures.

Another windfall came the next year when upon distribution of $140,000 held by the Artists' Fund Society, Edward Gay, a member for sixteen years, received $2,304.

Gay got good notices in the papers. The *Daily Graphic*, as noted, reproduced *Broad Acres*; on April 2, 1888 the same newspaper reproduced his entry in the 63rd Annual Exhibition of the National Academy of Design. On February 27, 1888 the following appeared:

> "I shiver to tell you what I am at now" writes Edward Gay from Mount Vernon to an acquaintance in town. "When it is not too awful cold you can find me at work upon a canvas four feet by six, down on the salt marshes, trying to represent the effect of high tide on the salt

meadows. The idea I wish to convey is that at high tide the whole country looks as if it were sinking out of sight. I will try to give it that gloom which such a thought would naturally suggest. I shall call it 'Atlantis' —for one of the Spring exhibitions."

This is another example of the skill with which Edward Gay understood how to get his name in the newspapers. The "gloom" that he put into the piece was surely gratuitous— he never purposely put any gloom into any picture. Nor was he one to paint the mystical or the fanciful. His art directly represented what he saw. He thought that a picture should depict, should show the landscape. The high-flown idea was good for getting a note into the newspaper, but he knew well enough that for him it should not spill over into his painting.

Though unable to get the N.A. that he so much wanted, Edward Gay had many loyal friends among the older men who were powers in the National Academy. In 1887 T. Addison Richards was Secretary of the Academy, and he wrote a nice note "sending my congratulations upon your honors at the Prize exhibition. Your laurels have been well won, and I heartily hope that many more and yet brighter ones await you." Richards, born 1820, was one of the older men of the Hudson River School of which Gay never considered himself a part. Richards was succeeded at the Academy by C. S. Farrington, and in 1893 Farrington wrote a friendly note "Re article in Albany paper on Wyant by Mrs. Gay," requesting a copy for the Academy files.

The tenth and last child arrived in February of 1886, and she was given the name Ingovar. The name came from Norway, of course; it was the name of a delightful child who came each day to watch the artist sketch when he was at Molde. Martha, the mother, was 44; the eldest son was twenty-one.

The $2,304 that Edward Gay received from the distribution of the assets of the Artists' Fund Society in 1883 was used in part to finance the building of the third-floor studio at Mount Vernon. This amounted to a complete rebuilding of the roof of the house, and it made a larger and vastly better work place than the artist had had before. It also provided a proper place for "first showings" and receptions. It was ready in time for the September 1889 wedding of the eldest daughter, Vivien, who abandoned her study of architecture at Cornell in order to get married. The bride had made her wedding dress of beige silk upon which were sewn thousands of tiny yellow shells picked up on the beach. The wedding at five o'clock was a large affair with many guests; there were almost a hundred friends at the wedding and the reception that lasted until ten. The hundred guests were properly wined and dined, so this was indeed a great affair. The parents of the bride were both in great spirits, but the father of the bride especially acted his brief part with memorable gaiety and aplomb.

It was early in the next year that, through his old friend William Arkell, Edward Gay was commissioned to illustrate an article in a magazine. The article was about Egypt, and the commission was to two artists, Gay and M. de Forest Bolmer, who were sent to Egypt with expenses paid. Bolmer was a young landscape painter, thirty-six years old at the time, whom Edward Gay had known but slightly prior to the trip. Unhappily Bolmer took along his young sister Estelle, who turned out to be a nice girl but a nuisance on a trip like this. A rough crossing on the *LaGascogne* of the French Line brought them to LeHavre early in March 1890. The Paris edition of the *New York Herald* had a note saying, "Mr. Edward Gay and M. de F. Bolmer, two New York artists, representatives of *Frank Leslie's Illustrated Paper* and the *Judge Publishing Company*, passed through Paris yesterday on their way to Egypt and the upper Nile. Miss Estelle Bolmer accompanies her brother on the trip. The party expect to be gone three months."

Several days were spent in Paris looking at pictures in the

Louvre and the Luxembourg. These visits to the galleries turned out to be the real highlight of the entire trip. Writing to Martha, Gay says, "The days in Paris were very full—saw many of the things twice so as to profit by leisure and have time to study the pictures. How very odd it is to see these fine pictures often; you alternate between rapture and disappointment. The great Rousseau and Delacroix in the Louvre affect me in this way particularly. The Rousseau was not nearly as good on this second visit—Mr. B. was also disappointed. The Delacroix were greater than ever—the "Don Juan Wreck," the small boat seen with 22 figures, was more terrible than ever. Mr. B. and I studied the landscape painters very closely—the great fault we had to find with most modern landscape was the sky. Mr. B. says I paint as good as the best, especially the sky" . . . It is somewhat surprising that Gay speaks of his young companion as Mr. B. after being with him for almost two weeks, but perhaps it was no more than a reflection of the formality of the times.

From Paris the party travelled by train to Nice, and then on to Rome for a few days and several days at Naples. Finally they took ship at Brindisi for Alexandria. In Cairo they were at Shepheard's Hotel, and found it very expensive, costing "15 dollars a day." Edward Gay says the heavy cost was due to "unfortunate management—I found out when it was too late that we could have lived nicely at a French Hotel for $2 a day." It was Miss Bolmer, "our little princess," who made them go to Shepheard's.

If the trip was scheduled to last for three months it appears to have been cut short, for after a week in Egypt they were back at Brindisi where the party separated, the Bolmers going to Venice and Gay taking a steamer to London. The letters home make it pretty clear that the little princess was a problem and that Edward Gay was happy to part from her. There was no hard feeling against the Bolmers, but just a sense of relief at parting.

This trip to Egypt was Edward Gay's only experience

with travel paid for because of work commissioned by a publisher, and it seems not to have been a very happy experience. In his letters there is no mention of doing any sketching or painting, nor do we have any indication that the proposed magazine articles ever came out. Search of the 1890-91 issues of *Leslie's* and *Judge* has failed to locate them. Edward Gay did make a number of good small pictures of sailboats on the Nile. One such picture has on the back of it a note in the handwriting of the artist:

> To Nell.
> The sun is the secret of the East,
> There is no light elsewhere.
> Geo. Wm. Curtis

Before starting on the trip to Egypt an exhibition and sale had been worked up with the old friends at Annersley's in Albany. Like all travellers, however, Edward Gay forgot about mundane affairs. He wrote to Martha from Brindisi, "You notice I avoid saying anything about the Albany sale—I am in another world, I suppose, and do not care." Well, Martha cared. This letter was forwarded to her in care of Annersley and Co., 57 N. Pearl St., Albany, where she had gone to look out for their interests.

At this time Edward Gay was serving on the Selection Committee of the National Academy of Design, and several artists that wanted to have their pictures hung "on the line" wrote to him asking that he vote for their pictures. One such wrote, "I have had occasion to say a good many nice things of your pictures in the past, and if you can favor me in this matter I shall be forced to like the artist quite as well as the pictures, which is saying a good deal." Clairvoyance is not needed to conclude that this artist did not further his cause.

It was in October of 1890 that the *Chronicle*, the Mount Vernon weekly, noted: "On Monday evening last, Mr. Edward Gay again gave the Village one of his pleasant 'first views'." The new studio provided a place for such affairs. Joseph Wood, the Superintendent of Schools, was also editor of the *Chronicle,* and he was a friend to be invited and could be counted on for a suitable piece in the paper. Publicity, even in his home village, was important and valuable to our artist, and he seems always to have had notices in the newspapers. In the New York papers these came out fairly regularly. The *New York Herald* for March 29, 1901 reproduced "The Town Dock, Eastchester."

Edward Gay was honored by being made a life member of the Lotos Club, and the associations there meant much to him over many years. It was a policy of the club to ask the many artist members to loan pictures to be hung at the club. Thus Gay writes a note, "Mr. Wm. Macbeth will kindly let bearer have my picture 'The Quiet River' size 28" x 38" for the Lotos Club." It is good to note that he was painting smaller pictures. There was a long period in which he did many very large canvasses, and he always liked to do the big ones. His "Atlantis" was four feet by six feet, as were his "Hardanger Fjord" and the two "Black Creeks." "Left by the Tide" is three by five feet; the great Acropolis picture must have been five by nine. Who would buy such tremendous pictures? Who had houses big enough? The answer, of course, is that at the time the very large canvas was quite the thing, and there was a ready market and more money in the big ones. But the great Acropolis did not sell, and it stayed in the studio for many years. Finally, and this is unbelievable, in 1917 the U.S. Army advertised for big landscape paintings, and accepted this one as a gift to aid the war effort: the army used the picture to train artillerymen in range-finding. You can hear Edward Gay when he snorted,

> " 'There are more things in heaven and earth, Horatio,
> Than are dreamt of in your philosophy.' "

The work went on and many prizes were won. At the Pan American Exposition in Buffalo in 1901 Edward Gay won a bronze medal. In 1903 a much more substantial prize, a money prize, was taken by his "Miamus River"; this was the Shaw Purchase prize of the Society of American Artists. The next year his "Black Creek" took a bronze medal at the St. Louis Exposition. This picture is one of the few painted in South Carolina: Edward Gay said the land about Hartsville was "weary, stale, flat, and unprofitable," with the accent on the "flat." But the great thing was that at Hartsville he got canvas free. He painted upon the excellent though somewhat coarsely woven canvas used for dryer felt on the paper machine—his son-in-law was a paper manufacturer.

His first visit was in 1898, and he came fairly frequently afterwards, sometimes going on down to Florida. It was on the first visit that he was taken into the swamp of the upper reaches of Black Creek and he made a pencil sketch on which he wrote, "The River Styx, S.C., Dec. 30, 1898. Warm as an early June day. E. Gay." In January 1902 he wrote Macbeth, "Will you kindly look out for my interests: My address for a month or so will be Hartsville, S. Carolina. I will likely send you some sunshine from there." By February he was at Ormand, Florida, and he wrote again to Macbeth, "Your letter to Hartsville was forwarded to me here. I was lounging on the sand in the shade of a palm tree *fanning myself* when it was handed me. These particulars are given you with malicious intent, for I see by the papers that you have it very cold in New York!" It is evident that Edward Gay was basking also in his pride of affluence— much of it due to his connection with Macbeth, which continued upon a happy basis for many years. In March 1902, on his return home, he wrote,

Dear Mr. Macbeth,
    I endeavored to stand up under the surprise, as well

as the pleasure, your kind note and enclosure caused me.

I am inclined to say some nice things on this occasion, but let it suffice that your prompt as well as kindly act has cemented a friendship which must be advantageous to us both.

Sincerely yours,
Edward Gay

In nearby Bronxville lived the successful and wealthy old friend Frank R. Chambers, who had come up from Alabama, and who was responsible for the great success of Rogers Peet Company, the men's clothing stores. Edward Gay called often at Crow's Nest, the Chambers' great house on a hill, and he had sold a number of landscapes that hung there. He did not often buy anything from Rogers Peet, but he built an image for himself with his costume. This was always the same: a grey suit, a white shirt with wing collar and a soft yellowed-silk bow tie, and a wide-brimmed grey felt hat, somewhat Western in feeling. Since he painted outside much of the time, this hat was essential to shade his eyes from the sun and to keep his long hair from blowing in the wind. He was very proud of a new hat, the same as always, that he had got at Rogers Peet, and he went to call on Mr. Chambers. The story is told by a daughter of the house:

A delightful friend of my parents, back in the 90's was the landscape painter, Mr. Edward Gay. He wore the traditional artist's slouch hat of soft gray felt with a wide brim, and hunched his tall lean body into an old gray suit, summer and winter.

One of his sons was a clever artist in many media, as original as his parent. He had found a calico pony of Western origin and hitched him to a skeleton buggy without a top and with a single seat.

One sunny afternoon, my family was astonished to

see Mr. Gay drive up the long hill to our house in this remarkable vehicle, for they had recently learned he was suffering from lumbago. Mr. Gay climbed slowly out of the wagon and tied the pony's check-rein to the ring of a wrought-iron stanchion in front of the house, under a big hickory tree.

The family welcomed him heartily as he seated himself carefully in a rocking chair on the porch.

The little pony soon became restless. He jerked the check-rein nervously and moved the light carriage from side to side; suddenly he was free. He whirled around and started down the hill.

With unbelievable speed, Mr. Gay leapt from his chair on the porch and ran down the front steps into the road. He almost grasped the pony's bridle but the pony shook him off. Mr. Gay fell and rolled over and over in the dusty road, crushing his famous hat beyond repair.

My parents were very anxious as they ran to pick him up, dust him off and inquire about his bad back. Mr. Gay shrugged off all their questions and asked to be taken home.

My father ordered his own buggy to be hitched up. He helped Mr. Gay up into it and went off down the hill to find the runaway. On his return, Father reported that they found the pony grazing quietly by the roadside with the wagon intact, and that Mr. Gay had insisted on driving himself home.

My father's business was men's clothing, so as soon as he reached his office on Monday, he ordered a gray felt hat for Mr. Gay, as nearly as possible like the old one.

Days went by and no word came from the Gays by mail or personal call. Father was puzzled that something had gone wrong. But one day, the round gray pasteboard box in which he had sent Mr. Gay's hat appeared like magic.

Father opened it slowly and gave a shout of laughter. Mr. Gay had made a wooden circle which fitted snugly into the bottom of the box. On it he had tacked one of the loveliest oil sketches he ever painted. It was the deep blue water of Long Island Sound with two dark rocks at one side and the hazy mist and warm sunshine of a perfect summer morning beyond.

For the rest of his very long life, my father kept this picture on the wall of his bedroom. He never ceased to enjoy it and the friendship of the Gays.

And Mr. Gay never had a twinge of lumbago for the rest of his very long life.

The George Inness Gold Medal, awarded by the National Academy of Design was won in 1905—a fine achievement, but Edward Gay still was not a full member of the Academy. He still had to sign himself A.N.A.: "Associate of the National Academy"; and at age 68 this was a vexation. The Inness Gold Medal was a fine thing, really heavy, solid gold—it must have weighed at least 4 oz. (worth some $350 today) —all in a grand Tiffany box, and with a gold-plated plaster replica so that the obverse, with bas-relief head of George Inness, done by Hartley in 1900, could be displayed at the same time as the reverse, inscribed, "In memory of George Inness, given by his son, awarded by the National Academy of Design to Edward Gay, 1905." The head of Inness is so much like Edward Gay that one would think them brothers.

Edward Gay had just about abandoned all hope of ever getting the N.A. when in May 1907 the coveted honor finally was dropped into his mailbox, signed by his friend Harry W. Watrous, Corresponding Secretary. It read,

Sir:
I have the pleasure to inform you that you have been duly elected an

ACADEMICIAN . . . .

Well, finally it had come, and he accepted it with good grace, though inside it seemed bitter indeed that the long-expected should have come at such long last, when he was seventy years old.

His friends in Mt. Vernon celebrated his success: by "popular subscription" (worked up by Mr. Wood, of course), his "Taormina" picture was given to the Mt. Vernon Public Library. It was in 1924, some seventeen years later, that his two lunettes, expressly painted for the high-arched foyer, were presented to the library by the Westchester Women's Club. Though poorly lit, these may be seen today. One is the Acropolis, the other Mt. Etna, with ruins in the foreground. The latter is the better of the two. The Taormina panel is beneath.

A one-man show was presented at Clausen Galleries, 7 East 35th Street, in December of 1908. The catalog lists thirty-one paintings and has a foreword by Arthur Hoeber:

> To follow a congenial profession, to merit the esteem and affection of one's fellow workers, to receive official recognition and to have sufficient material encouragement in the practice of the arts to have all the necessities of life and a few of the luxuries is to be blessed above the ordinary man. Few obtain as much, none obtain more. All these conditions have been vouchsafed Edward Gay, the Landscape Painter, who offers here, at Mr. Clausen's Gallery, a sort of retrospective display, for though he needs no introduction to that part of the public who follow art matters, memories are proverbially short and it is well now and then to call a halt and demand a little introspection, as well as some retrospection . . .

Arthur Hoeber was at once an artist and a critic. He wrote regularly for the papers; his painting was good enough to make Edward Gay propose his name for Academy membership. Beyond this, he was a good friend who would gladly write a nice piece for the catalog of Edward Gay's showing at age seventy-one.

Chapter XI

*Art is long, and time is fleeting,
And our hearts, though stout and brave,
Still, like muffled drums, are beating
Funeral marches to the grave.*
     —LONGFELLOW

As is usual, perhaps, it was the wife who persuaded and cajoled. Or it may be that Martha found the money, bought the land, and built the little summer place at Cragsmoor. It was an artists' colony, to be sure, and many of Edward Gay's old friends were there. In any event, the little house was built, with a spring-house at the front door and a broad view over the valley and toward the Catskills. The ever-resourceful son Duncan helped to get the house built, and then built separately and down the slope from the house a small whitewashed studio with good north window, and even running water conducted in a pipe from a small dam in the brook. This water falling constantly into a basin hollowed from a log made a pleasant sound that hid the outside noises from the house; this water was most useful too for the daily rite of washing paint brushes, always meticulously done by the artist himself.

Victor Hugo says, "There are fathers who do not love their children; there is no grandfather who does not love his grandson." Our artist had but one grandson. The difference in their ages was some sixty years, so it was the more remarkable that there developed between the boy and his grandfather a rapport and understanding that was most satisfying to each. This could be described as a friendship: it was valued accordingly. At age twelve or thirteen the boy spent a summer at Cragsmoor and the old man was friendly and kind. He set out to get acquainted with his grandson and to win him over. They sat together in the little whitewashed studio below the house. The old man talked of reading, Shakespeare, and of the Bible. He could quote long passages, and he urged the boy to memorize. He also encouraged the boy and told him to study hard at the Latin he was just beginning in school; he said that Latin was good, but that Greek was even more important.

On other visits to the house at Mt. Vernon there was less opportunity for intimate meetings, but he would call down from the studio that "the boy" was to be sent up to him. It was understood that they were not to be interrupted; thus the lessons would go on. The boy did not know then that they were lessons, but in after years he understood that the old man was teaching him and guiding him toward especially cherished knowledge. Greece was always a theme to be returned to again and again. There were passages from Gilbert Murray's Euripides, with discussions of meaning and of art. The old man came back often to the stories of the Olympic Games, especially the running of the relay race; and the passing of the torch—actually just a stick, he said—the passing of the torch was a saying that came later. Entranced, the boy did not realize that he was receiving a torch, albeit a small one, from the old runner finishing his part in the race.

The story now to be told is of a visit that came much later when the grandson was eighteen years old, and becoming a man. On climbing the stair to the third floor he found his grandfather seated on the rug-covered couch beneath the north window. Although the old man seemed old, old and decrepit, the remembered easy rapport was still there and brought the two to an understanding which was quiet and pleasant.

After they had sat a while the light faded in the winter dusk and the old man said with a frankness that might have been lugubrious, but was not, "I am very old, and I have only a little time to tell you things that I want you to know." He took a book from the shelf at the end of the couch, and reaching behind the books he brought out a bottle of whisky. This was in Prohibition days, and such a prize was not easy to come by, nor should it be wasted. He poured two drinks into small glasses that foresight had provided, and he said, "I know you are young to do it, but I want you to have a drink with me, and there may not be many chances. I want you to know that whisky is good and that you must not believe those Baptists in South Carolina who say it is not! Whisky *is* good."

Whereupon they drank to that, together.

The *New York Herald* for September 15, 1912 has a page of pictures of artists at Cragsmoor: "Mr. Edward Gay, working outdoors; Mr. Carleton Wiggins, at Central Valley; Mr. George Inness, on the steps below his pergola; Mr. C. C. Curman, making an outdoor study; and Mr. E. L. Henry, in his studio." From the Cragsmoor happy days there is also the large sketch in oil, done by Arthur I. Keller, showing Gay painting out of doors, the canvas askew on the easel, and the landscape on the canvas more askew, the bottle of whisky lying on the grass. Keller was an illustrator and a fine draftsman, and this large sketch is an excellent likeness, full of fun withal.

There are many portraits of Edward Gay, for he was eminently paintable. The portrait by J. D. Blondell, presented to the National Academy in 1869 when Gay was made associate, is sadly deteriorated, but obviously a likeness. The N. R. Brewer portrait, done in 1910, with hat, is strong and vigorous. The portrait done at Cragsmoor by Augusta Sturtevant has Gay painting outdoors, shading his eyes with his hand as he looks into the sun. But perhaps the best portrait is the one done in 1898 by T. W. Wood, then the president of the National Academy. Although somewhat too round-faced, it looks much like Edward Gay in his years of maturity before the strong evidences of age appeared.

The house at Cragsmoor was built in 1905, somewhat against his will; but Edward Gay always went along with Martha's enthusiasm and he soon grew to love the place. The two of them were there every summer for many years. There were wonderful friends and much good talk. There too they entertained their grandchildren, although the little red cottage was pretty primitive. There is a story of the visit of the eldest granddaughter, who brought with her a South Carolina cousin. This lovely young girl had recently lost her mother, and she wore only the long black dresses of mourning decreed by the custom in the South. The two girls were almost nineteen, full of fun and gaiety, and Edward Gay enjoyed them greatly, but he told Martha she would have to get Ruth out of those horrible dresses. Martha was easily successful in this, and the mourning was put aside. The artist, as he sallied forth with paintbox, easel and canvas in the morning, would pose a question, usually a literary question, which the girls were to answer upon his return. This proved great intellectual fun and was long remembered.

Nowadays, when so many men retire at sixty-five or seventy, it is good to recall that some of the artist's best work was done after he was seventy-five. In March of 1914 he had a one-man show at McDonough Art Gallery, 20 West 34th Street. He exhibited thirty-three paintings. Again the catalog contained a foreword by Arthur Hoeber. In 1919, when Edward Gay was 82, pictures were assembled for a one-man show at Eckhart Gallery in Hartford, Connecticut; and in that year, too, Rose Gallery in New York listed twelve of his paintings for sale. Sales must have been fairly good and health fairly good too, for at age eighty-two Edward Gay returned to Athens to view again the home of Pericles and Asphasia. Martha went with him.

When his first great-grandchild was born, Gay was greatly cheered. He got the train to New York and went striding along Fifth Avenue, confident he would encounter some acquaintance. Sure enough, he met old Dolph, who asked, "What's new?"

Gay replied, "I am the great-grandfather of a Virginian!"

Visiting his son Duncan at Redding, Connecticut, he was taken to call on Samuel Clemens, who lived nearby. On hearing that his visitor was a landscape painter, old Mark Twain gestured toward his big window and said, "That is my picture; I need no other." Edward Gay was enraged.

For the Centennial Exhibition of the National Academy of Design in 1925 at the Corcoran Gallery in Washington (Oct. 17 to Nov. 18) and at the Grand Central Art Galleries in New York (Dec. 1, 1925 to Jan 3, 1926) Edward Gay's painting "Cragsmoor" was included. At the Corcoran it was well hung in a small room with two other pictures, a Frank A. Bicknell and an R. M. Shurtleff.

A story of this period illustrates the happy congeniality between Edward Gay and his son Will, the judge, who lived with him in the house at Mt. Vernon. The talk of the time was of the French psychologist Émile Coué who was advocating the great power of auto-suggestion and recommended that one should say, when ill, "I am getting better and better every day in every way." Edward Gay came into the library and reported that he was very, very ill. (He had a cold). The judge gave him no sympathy, but suggested that he try the advice of Coué. The old gentleman responded that there was not time enough. He said, "You want me to tell my beads and say, 'Oh, Hell, I'm well!'"

The story of the death of Edward Gay was told by his daughter Dorothy. She went in to check on him, and to say good night. He was propped high on his pillows. He said to her, "My dear, the jig is up. You'd best call your brother." She called Will, and he came at once and gave him a few drops of paregoric for sleep, then sat beside the bed with his hand on the old man's shoulder. Edward Gay did fall asleep; he did not waken.

O'Toole Library
Withdrawn